TEACHERS AND WRITINGS

History	Approximate dates A.D.	Writings
Jesus Christ	B.C. 4–A.D. 29	
Church in Roman Empire	100 – – –	*New Testament fixed*
Jewish Dispersion	70–135	*Talmud begun*
Buddhism in China	70 – – –	*Lotus scripture*
Zoroastrian religion of Persia	220–700	*Later Avesta*
Mohammed	570–632	*Koran*
Islam from Spain to India	632–732	*Moslem traditions*
Church in England and N. Europe	600 – – –	
Buddhism in Tibet and Japan	600 – – –	*Shinto Chronicles*
Chan (Zen) Buddhism in China	600 – – –	*Zen texts*
East and West churches separate	1053	
Friars, Francis, Dominic	1220 – – –	
Nanak and Sikhs	1469–1538	*Granth scriptures*
Reformation and Counter-Reform	1520 – – –	
Anglicans and Independents separate	1662	
Methodist revival	1738 – – –	
Anglo-Catholic revival	1833 – – –	
Jewish Reform synagogues	1842 – – –	
Bab martyred, Bahais founded	1850 – – –	*Bahai writings*
Salvation Army	1865 – – –	
Shinto revival, Buddhism separated	1868	*Shinto sect writings*
Hindu Ramakrishna mission	1897	
Moslem Caliph abolished	1924	
Revival of Moslem and Buddhist missions		
Christian missions world-wide		

A BOOK OF

WORLD RELIGIONS

Books by the same author for further reading:

The World's Living Religions (Pan)
What World Religions Teach (Harrap)
Worship in the World's Religions (Faber & Faber).

A Book of

WORLD RELIGIONS

by

E. G. PARRINDER, D.D.

*Reader in the Comparative Study of Religions
in the University of London*

HULTON EDUCATIONAL PUBLICATIONS

©
1965
E. G. PARRINDER

ISBN 0 7175 0443 3

First published 1965 by Hulton Educational Publications Ltd.,
Raans Road, Amersham, Bucks
Reprinted 1967
Reprinted 1970
Reprinted 1972
Reprinted 1974
Reprinted 1976
Reprinted 1978
Printed Offset Litho in Great Britain by Cox & Wyman Ltd.,
London, Fakenham and Reading

CONTENTS

LIST OF PHOTOGRAPHS

PREFACE

This book aims at providing information about the religions of the modern world. They are introduced as activities in home and temples. Their story falls into four parts: Worship, the Founders, Holy Books and Teachings, Growth and Present State. Religion and culture are entwined, in their various forms, right across the world. Not only Religious Knowledge, but also History, Geography and World Affairs are illustrated by this study. Pictures, maps, charts and reading checks are included to light up the story and reinforce its description.

Acknowledgement is made for permission to quote from: *The Revised Standard Version of the Bible* (Nelson); *The Qur'ān Translated* by R. Bell (T. & T. Clark); *The Thirteen Principal Upanishads* by R. E. Hume (Oxford); *Sources of Indian Tradition*, ed. by W. T. de Bary (Columbia U.P.); *The Hymns of Zarathustra* by J. Duchesne-Guillemin (Murray); *Sacred Writings of the Sikhs* (Allen & Unwin); *The Analects of Confucius*, and *The Way and its Power*, by A. Waley (Allen & Unwin); *The Dhammapada* by S. Radhakrishnan (Oxford); *Sources of Japanese Tradition*, ed. by W. T. de Bary (Columbia U.P.); *Hindu Scriptures* by N. Macnicol (Dent, Everyman); *Bhagavad Gita*, translated by S. Radhakrishnan (Allen & Unwin); *Ashanti* by R. Rattray (Oxford University Press); *Buddhist Scriptures*, translated by E. Conze (Penguin).

Acknowledgement is also made to the following for the use of photographs not in the author's or publisher's copyright: The British Museum; The India Office Library (for the photograph of Nanak, reproduced by courtesy of the Secretary of State for Commonwealth Relations); J. Allan Cash; The Japanese Embassy; John Hillelson Agency; The Ministry of Works (Crown Copyright); Oxford University Press; Paul Popper Ltd.; Radio Times Hulton Picture Library; The Salvation Army; Shell Photographic Unit; Societa Editrice Libraria, Milan.

Part 1

MEN AT PRAYER

Every day, in every country, countless men and women give some time to thoughts of God or a spiritual being. They put their thoughts into words which are prayers and meditations.

Christians pray at home, or on Sundays and special occasions in a church. As they pray they are joined in a great invisible link with people of many races, colours and languages. In great cathedrals or in village chapels, in Eskimo igloos or in African forest huts, they say similar words and share the same faith. Jews at home or in the synagogue vow to love God and keep his commandments with all others who do the same.

But while these are joined together with those who believe as they do, there are millions of people who belong to different religions but who pray and meditate every day. The Moslem bows towards the holy city of Mecca and calls upon the name of Allah. The Hindu sitting cross-legged on the banks of the river Ganges calls upon the World Spirit to enlighten his mind. The Buddhist in Burma or Japan sits in thought trying to fathom the mystery of life. Many others, with various practices, think about 'human being, eternity and God'. They pray in different ways from us, but the purpose is much the same. This is what Kipling meant when he paraphrased a verse by Kabir, an Indian teacher:

My brother kneels (so saith Kabir)
   To stone and brass in heathen-wise,
But in my brother's voice I hear
   My own unanswered agonies.
His God is as his Fates assign —
His prayer is all the world's – and mine.

We should not today talk about a 'heathen', for that means a man of the 'heath', a 'pagan' or peasant. The great religions about which we are going to read were founded or directed by great thinkers, with a large store of wisdom. Because of the difficulties of travel in the past, our religions grew up separately. But today with easy communications many people from the West go to the East, and many from the East and Africa visit Europe and America. We meet one another, and not only for trade; we can learn about each other's religions and ideas. In this book we are trying to get an introduction to some of the most important living religions, and by words and pictures to enter into their ways.

Man is a religious being. For many ages he has tried to understand the universe and his own self. Even those who do not worship regularly in public may pray at home, in time of need, or think about the great problems of life. Here we are going to see what other people have thought about the meaning of life, what they have meant by a Creator, and the kind of life men should lead. We shall find some strange practices and curious teachings. But patience and tolerance are essential when learning about religion, for it is one of the most precious things of life. In dealing with religion, as the poet Yeats said about other thoughts, you must 'tread softly, because you tread on my dreams'.

11

THE MOSLEM CALL TO PRAYER

At daybreak, and four other times during the day, the prayer 'crier' goes up into a tower (minaret) or stands at the door of the mosque and calls in a loud voice that men and women should turn to prayer. The cry is always the same, right across the Moslem world, from Morocco in the west to Mongolia in the east. It is in the Arabic language and in translation it says:

God is most great. God is most great.
I bear witness that there is no God but God.
I bear witness that Mohammed is the Apostle of God.
Come to prayer. Come to salvation.

In the early morning the crier (*muezzin*) adds, 'Prayer is better than sleep.' The faithful can go to the mosque for prayer if they wish. The mosque is a 'place of prostration', surrounded by walls with open courts. In it people prostrate on prayer-mats, towards the direction of the Kaaba shrine in Mecca, which is marked by a niche in the wall.

The Star and the Crescent
Moon are on many flags
and domes of Islam

Many men, and all women, pray at home or wherever they may happen to be. The prayers are the same as those said in the mosque, for there is a fixed order. Preparation is made with water, by washing head and hands and feet. The prayer-mat is spread towards Mecca. Barefoot, the Moslem stands on the mat and begins prayers from the holy book, the Koran. He begins with the words, 'In the name of God, the Merciful, the Compassionate', followed by several

A mosque in Nigeria

12

A minaret

13

short chapters of the Koran. He prostrates, touching the ground with his forehead, and says, 'God is most great.' This order is repeated, and the formal prayer is over. But personal prayers are added. Prayers are made five times a day: at dawn, midday, afternoon, evening and night.

This religion is called Islam, meaning 'submission', or 'surrender' to the will of God. The follower is a Moslem, which comes from the same root word. He is a surrendered man who tries to live according to the will of God. In the West he is often called a Mohammedan, but this name is disliked, as Mohammed is not worshipped. Moslems recognise that other people worship God in

their own way, particularly those who worship one God and have holy books, like Jews and Christians. But a Moslem believes that Mohammed was the greatest Prophet of God, though Moses and Jesus are honoured also.

Most Moslems observe the five daily times of prayer faithfully, though in the business of modern life two or more acts of prayer may be joined together. It is an impressive sight to see the Moslem unroll his mat wherever he is, by the roadside, in the market, at the railway station, or on board ship. On Fridays all male Moslems should join together in the mosque for communal prayer to God. This is not a day of complete

14

rest, and shops are only closed during the prayer at the midday hour. The mosques of the Moslem world are often beautiful buildings, with open courtyards and a tank or fountain in the middle. Minaret towers stand in the front wall or at the corners. A covered sanctuary contains the niche for the prayer direction, and a pulpit for sermons.

At Friday prayers a teacher or leader gives a short address on verses from the Koran or some topical subject, with exhortations to good conduct. In the mosque there are no images of any kind, no paintings or pictorial windows, for Moslems dislike all representation of human form. But texts in Arabic are written on the walls, and there is fine

Courtyard of a mosque

15

fretwork on the pulpit and stone or marble trellises on the windows. There are no priests or paid religious leaders, and so there is no collection of money for their support in the mosque service, but all Moslems are supposed to give alms to the poor.

In the mosque there are no seats or pews, since the floor is covered at prayer times with prayer-carpets, often with beautiful patterns, of which the Persian carpets are famous. At other times the floor is usually uncovered, and may be of marble with mosaic patterns. There are no hymns or music during the services, but outside the mosque music may be used for ordinary or religious festivals.

Apart from the prayer times people may go to the mosque for private prayer, and strangers are usually allowed in if they remove their shoes at the door. Women may go for private prayer, and in some places now they are being allowed to take their place in public prayer behind the men. But they always pray at home, and treasure their faith which brings trust in God. Special prayers are said in time of need, and many people use prayer-beads to assist in the repetition of devotions, like the recital of ninety-nine 'Beautiful Names' of God. Special preachers may come in time of festival, but normally the Koran is taught in schools and learnt by heart in the Arabic language.

Other important buildings are the tombs of Moslem saints and religious leaders (sheiks), and there are many of these in the Moslem world. Here people come to ask the intercession of the saint at special times, or to hold a feast on the date of his birthday. Relics of the saints, including some of Mohammed himself, his clothing, and Korans belonging to some of his followers, are treasured. Other festivals and further religious and social duties of Moslems will be mentioned in a later chapter.

For more about Islam turn to pages 60, 100, 147.

JEWISH HOME AND SYNAGOGUE

On the doorpost of many a Jewish home and room is a small box (mezuzah) which contains a small piece of parchment. On this are written words from the holy book, the Bible, including the verses which say, 'thou shalt bind them for a sign upon thy hand, and they shall be for frontlets between thine eyes. And thou shalt write them upon the doorposts of thy house, and upon thy gates.'

When members of the family go in and out of the door they often touch and kiss the scripture box, so as to remember the law of God. The box shows that the house is Jewish; it shows also that it is a holy place, the home as well as the synagogue, where prayer to God is made regularly. Some modern Jews do not use prayer boxes, but they still maintain that the home is blessed by God.

The daily prayers of a Jew are laid down in a Prayer Book, and are similar to longer ones used at the weekly Sabbath. There are prayers for the morning, and prayers before retiring at night. There is grace said before and after meals. Private prayers are made for special needs. But all the more important and regular prayers include the verse, 'Hear (Shema), O Israel.' In some ways this is like the Moslem call to prayer, and it goes thus:

Hear, O Israel: the Lord our God, the Lord is One.
And thou shalt love the Lord thy God with all thy heart, and with all thy soul, and with all thy might.

This is found in the Bible (Deuteronomy 6:4–9), and it was first addressed to the Children of Israel when they came out of bondage in Egypt and made their way to the Holy Land. All down the ages, in their many troubles and persecutions, the Jews have held to faith in one God. This belief in one God came to be the basis also of Christianity and Islam.

The Jewish weekly holy day is the Sabbath, meaning 'rest'. It is a day when no work is done, and the stricter Jews refuse to

Six-pointed Star of David

Sabbath Lights

travel, use money or touch the phone on the Sabbath. Since the days are counted from sunset to sunset, the Saturday Sabbath begins at dusk on the Friday.

The Sabbath begins with the mother of the house saying a blessing over candles, in special highly polished candlesticks. The husband and children gather round her, and as she lights the candles she says: 'Blessed art thou, O Lord our God, King of the Universe, who hast sanctified us by thy commandments, and commanded us to kindle the Sabbath light.' The father takes a cup of wine, says a blessing over it and then everyone takes a sip. Then the Sabbath loaf is sliced and shared. After that an evening meal may follow.

Jewish public services are held in the synagogue. This word comes from Greek, from the time when the ancient Jews were under Greek rule, from the fourth century

B.C. It means simply a place of 'bringing together'. Synagogues are plain buildings like the chapels of the Free Churches. Inside there is little decoration, though some of the modern ones have some stained glass windows with designs of the six-pointed star, the rolls of the Law, or the seven-branched candlesticks from the ancient temple. There are pews across the synagogue, and a gallery upstairs in which women sit in the older Orthodox synagogues. The modern Liberal or Reform Jews allow all the family to sit together.

At the end of the synagogue is a reading-desk, and behind it a cupboard or recess called the Ark, covered by doors or curtains. In the Ark are kept rolls of the Law, the first five books of the Bible. This is the Law (Torah) or Pentateuch (five books). In front of the Ark hangs a lamp. In some modern synagogues there is also an organ and a

17

choir for singing. On the wall is a panel bearing the first words of the Ten Commandments, in square Hebrew letters.

Men usually wear hats or skull caps during the service, and prayer-shawls round their shoulders. There is a Reader who recites prayers and a minister or Rabbi ('master') who preaches a sermon.

The synagogue service begins with prayers and praises of God, and especially the Eighteen Blessings (Amidah) which thank God for his care and pray for the restoration of the service of his house. The chief point of the service is the procession and reading of the Law. The Ark is opened, and it is seen to be brightly lit inside. A scroll is taken out, which is covered in a velvet or silk robe lavishly decorated and crowned with gold or silver. It is carried all round the syna-gogue, and as it passes everybody bows or touches it, and turns round so that nobody has his back to the Law. Then it is taken up to the reading-desk, the cover removed, and the scroll held up for everybody to see. Then a lesson is read from the Law, in the Hebrew language, though it may also be read in translation in English or whatever the language of the country may be. A lesson from later parts of the Bible, such as the Prophets, may also be read.

Any lay person may stand up to read the lessons, and boys (and sometimes girls) read it first at the time of their thirteenth birthday. A sermon may follow, with more prayers and hymns, but there is no collection of money in the synagogue.

There are special festivals of the Jewish year, which recall great events in their

Reading the Law

18

Scrolls in covers

history: Passover, to commemorate how God 'passed over' and delivered the Hebrews at the Exodus, and Tabernacles, when people decorate rooms with branches like booths to remember their days in the desert. Others recall the deliverance by the Maccabees and Esther. But most important are the ceremonies of the New Year and the Day of Atonement. This is a time of repentance for sin, and special services, based on services in the Bible (Leviticus 16). It is the greatest time of Jewish social gathering, when shops are closed, and family and synagogue prayers most widely held.

For more about Jews, turn to pages 52, 88, 140.

19

CHRISTIAN CHURCHES AND SERVICES

Perhaps most of the readers of this book are Christians, or know something about one or two of the churches. But there are other churches and services that need some description. And then there will be some readers who live in other lands and follow another religion, and they may be glad of an introduction to Christianity.

Christians believe that Jesus of Nazareth (whose life will be described on page 56) was the Christ ('anointed' of God, or Messiah). They were first called Christians at Antioch in Syria (Acts 11:26) in the first century. Christians believe in one God, like Jews and Moslems, but they believe that God is best and fully revealed in Jesus Christ and in his Spirit, and this complex belief in God is expressed in the teaching of the Trinity.

There are many differences between the kinds of worship practised in the various churches. But all Christians use the prayer

The Cross recalls the Crucifixion of Jesus. The three letters are an abbreviation of his name in Greek.

given by Jesus which begins:

Our Father, which art in heaven.

This is given in full on page 25. Other prayers and praises differ considerably. But most churches use the Apostles' Creed (page 135) or a longer statement of faith. In private prayer some of these, and other prayers from a Prayer Book, may be used, with additional prayers for special needs. Some Christians recite prayers with the help

A Parish Church

of a 'rosary' or prayer-beads, as many people of other religions do, such as Moslems and Hindus. These prayers are most frequently 'Our Father' (*Pater noster*) and 'Hail Mary' (*Ave Maria*).

The Christian holy day is Sunday, when shops are closed, though amusements are not so restricted now as they used to be. The main church services are said then. A church (from a Greek word, 'Lord's house') is often the most beautiful building in a village or town, and some are very ancient. Buildings of some churches may be called chapels, originally meaning special or additional places of worship.

The Sunday morning and evening services in the Church of England or Protestant Episcopal or Lutheran Churches generally are made up of hymns, prayers, Bible readings, creed, and sermon. There is a choir robed in white and the priest or minister in charge wears a white surplice over a black cassock or long robe. In the Free or Reformed Churches the service is much the same, but the prayers are not usually read or fixed, but are adapted for the occasion. There are more hymns, and fewer fixed chants, no creed, and perhaps a choir in plain dress.

For Roman Catholics and most Christians there are special Sacraments ('sacred' mysteries). Protestants recognise two of these: Baptism and Communion. Roman Catholics and Eastern Orthodox hold five more rites as Sacraments: Confirmation, Marriage, Ordination, Penance, Unction. The first three of these are used by Protestants, but are not put on the same level as what they call the 'Sacraments of the Gospel', namely, Baptism and Communion.

Baptism means bathing or sprinkling with water. It is the sign of becoming a Christian, practised by the great majority of Christians. The Baptists immerse adults only, fully into water. Other Christians sprinkle water on children in baptism, though in tropical countries adult converts may be fully immersed.

The Holy Communion is so called because

Presbyterian morning service

Baptism at a Font

21

Roman Catholic Mass

it is taken as a Communion or fellowship with Christ, and it is held in memory of his death on the Cross. Sometimes it is called the Eucharist ('thanksgiving'), or Mass (from a word of 'dismissal'). Or, more simply, it is called the Lord's Supper or the Last Supper, because it has been observed ever since the Last Supper which Jesus held with his disciples. Under its many forms this service is special to Christians, as it marks the greatest occasion in their history.

In many churches and cathedrals the Communion or Mass is said at an altar lit with candles and marked with a plain Cross, or a Crucifix which bears an image of Christ. There are many prayers and chants, either in the language of the country, or in Latin or Greek. Portions are read from the Bible: Gospel and Epistle. Creeds are chanted. A cup (chalice) and plate (paten) of silver bear the bread (or wafer) and wine which stand for the broken body and blood of Jesus. These are blessed and then eaten, by priest and people. In the Roman Catholic church the wafer only is received by the lay people.

Communion is held daily in some churches, weekly or monthly in others. The Quakers (Friends) and Salvation Army do not have any sacraments, but they hold to the chief teachings of the creeds and believe that God is present in spirit at all services.

The Christian Year begins at Advent ('coming') four Sundays before Christmas, when the coming of Jesus is remembered, culminating in the services of Christmas (December 25), an old word meaning Christ-mass, the special Communion held on the birthday of Jesus. It is followed by Epi-phany, the 'showing' of the baby Jesus to the Wise Men, on January 6. Then comes Lent, 'spring', which prepares by fasting or self-denial for the memory of the last days of Jesus. Palm Sunday recalls his entry to Jerusalem, Good Friday the day of his Crucifixion, and Easter ('dawn') for his Resurrection. This is held at the time of the Jewish Passover, for Jesus was crucified then. Another Jewish feast, Pentecost ('fiftieth' day after the Passover), or Whitsun, is so called because of the white gowns worn by people who were baptized then; it cele-brates the coming of the Holy Spirit on the first apostles (Acts 2). So the whole Christian Year revolves round the historical events of the life of Christ and these are central to Christian faith.

For more about Christians, turn to pages 56, 94, 143, 172.

CHECK YOUR READING

What is a Moslem?
How many times a day does he pray?
Why does a Moslem prostrate himself?
How much of the Call to Prayer could a Christian say?
What is the Moslem holy day?
In what direction do Moslems turn in prayer?
How many Beautiful Names of God are there?
Where do Moslem women pray?
What is a Jewish prayer-box?
What is inside it?
What is the meaning of the word Sabbath?
How does the Sabbath begin?

What is a synagogue?
What is kept in the Ark?
What is the Law?
What does the Passover commemorate?
How is the Day of Atonement kept?
Where were Christians first called by this name?
What prayer did Jesus teach his disciples?
What is the Christian holy day?
What is a Sacrament?
How many Sacraments are there?
What does Baptism mean?
What does Communion celebrate?
Name the special days of the Christian Year.

SOME GREAT PRAYERS

The Opening, chapter one of the Koran, repeated at least ten times every day by all devout Moslems

In the Name of God, the Merciful, the Compassionate.
Praise be to God, the Lord of the worlds,
The Merciful, the Compassionate.
King on the Day of Judgement.
Thee do we serve and on thee do we call for help.
Guide us on the straight path,
The path of those to whom thou hast been gracious,
Not of those upon whom anger falls, or those who go astray.

The Men, last chapter of the Koran, repeated daily

In the Name of God, the Merciful, the Compassionate.
Say: I take refuge with the Lord of men,
The King of men, the God of men,
From the evil of the whispering, the lurking,
Which whispers in the hearts of men,
From among spirits and men.

JEWISH

From the Amidah (18 Blessings)

O Lord, open thou my lips, and my mouth shall declare thy praise.
Blessed art thou, O Lord our God and God of our Fathers, God of
Abraham, God of Isaac, and God of Jacob, the great, mighty and
revered God, the most high God, who bestowest lovingkindnesses
and possessest all things; who rememberest the pious deeds of the
patriarchs, and in love wilt bring a redeemer to their children's children
for thy name's sake.

Psalm 23

The Lord is my shepherd; I shall not want.
He maketh me to lie down in green pastures;
He leadeth me beside the still waters.
He restoreth my soul;
He guideth me in straight paths for his name's sake.
Yea, though I walk through the valley of the shadow of death,
I will fear no evil, for thou art with me;
Thy rod and thy staff, they comfort me.
Thou preparest a table before me, in the presence of my enemies;
Thou hast anointed my head with oil; my cup runneth over.
Surely goodness and mercy shall follow me all the days of my life;
And I will dwell in the house of the Lord for ever.

CHRISTIAN

The Lord's Prayer, taught by Jesus

Our Father, which art in heaven,
Hallowed be thy name; thy kingdom come;
Thy will be done, in earth as it is in heaven.
Give us this day our daily bread.
And forgive us our trespasses,
As we forgive them that trespass against us.
And lead us not into temptation, but deliver us from evil.
For thine is the kingdom, the power and the glory,
For ever and ever.

Opening prayer of the Communion, Book of Common Prayer

Almighty God, unto whom all hearts are open, all desires known, and
from whom no secrets are hid: Cleanse the thoughts of our hearts
by the inspiration of thy Holy Spirit, that we may perfectly love thee,
and worthily magnify thy holy name; through Christ our Lord.

A Church Choir

HINDU DEVOTION

The three religious groups that we have been describing: Christians, Jews and Moslems, are fairly close together. Their religions began in the same or neighbouring countries: Palestine and Arabia. Some of their beliefs are the same, though others are very different. They all practise social worship, as well as private prayers.

When we look farther east things change and customs are still more different. India is a great source of religious belief, and some religious ideas went from India to the farthest parts of Asia. Most people in India practise a religion that is called Hindu, which simply means Indian religion. It is a very old collection of many kinds of religious practices. One striking thing about the Hindus is that they worship, or use the names of, many gods and they have countless images of them. At the same time all learned men say that these are just different ways of speaking of the one Spirit, who is called Brahman. Another striking thing is that worship is individual. Prayer is performed alone, at home, on a river bank, or in a temple. Only occasionally are there great festivals when people gather together for common worship.

Indian society is divided into classes, called 'castes'. The kind of prayer varies from caste to caste. We shall look first at the worship of the higher castes, the priests (Brahmins) and others. Every devout Hindu recites a favourite prayer when he awakes each day, and many times during the day. It is taken from the ancient Veda scriptures, and is called 'the Mother of the Vedas':

Let us meditate upon the most excellent
    light of the radiant sun;
May he guide our minds.

Having repeated this prayer, the Hindu also utters the special name of God that he uses in worship, perhaps the god Vishnu or Shiva. He calls to mind the name of his religious teacher, and then says a prayer of

OM, a sacred Hindu word
used in meditation

remembrance in which he resolves to do his day's work in union with God. In fact he tries to identify himself with God, to be no different from him. He says: 'I am the Lord in no wise different from him, the Brahman. I suffer from no pains or ills. I am existence and knowledge and bliss, ever free. O Lord of the world, all intelligence, the greatest God, O Vishnu, as I awake early in the morning I shall fulfil all the duties of my daily life.'

The Hindu then takes a bath, binds up the tuft of hair on the top of his head, and recites again the verse of the Mother of the Vedas. As he performs his worship he is bare to the waist and barefoot. He wears a sacred thread over the left shoulder across the body to the waist. He makes marks on his face or body with paste or ash, varying with different gods. Morning prayer is said, either on a river bank, or in a worship room in the house before images or stone symbols. The Hindu sits, facing east, sprinkles water round himself and on the image. His chief concern is to fix his thoughts in meditation. To help in this he may repeat the name of God, or say the sacred verse tens or hundreds of times. Prayer-beads are also used to help in repetition and meditation. With a further water offering and bowing the prayer may end.

Another group of prayers is said before taking food, any time up to midday. This includes offering flowers, scent, incense, lights and food to the god of the image. Food is also given to guests, the poor and animals. A shorter act of worship is performed in the evening.

A Hindu at prayer

The use of images is very popular in India, but the image itself is not worshipped; it is taken as a sign of the spirit behind it. A great Hindu teacher said, 'One needs images and symbols, so long as God is not realised in his true form. It is God himself who has provided these various forms of worship to suit different stages of spiritual growth.'

Women and people of the lower castes use many images, of male or female gods, and of children. A favourite one is Krishna, who represents the great god Vishnu. In the most popular holy book of India, the Gita, Krishna says: 'If one of earnest spirit sets before me with devotion a leaf, a flower, fruit or water, I enjoy this offering of devotion.' One of the most impressive statues of the countless Hindu carvings is a great stone figure in a cave on an island near Bombay. This shows God with three faces, revealing his many natures as creator, destroyer and sustainer. This is taken as the one universal spirit, behind the many gods and images.

India is a land of great temples and statues. These are especially fine in the south; in the north the Moslems destroyed many temples and broke down their images because they disliked idolatry. But the great temples of south India are full of stone carvings, depicting the stories of gods and demons, kings and queens, and men and women in all occupations. The lavish stone carving can only be compared with the great stone statues on the Gothic cathedrals of Europe, and they date from about the same period. Other great Indian buildings, such as the Moslem Taj Mahal at Agra, which is a magnificent tomb, are more like the Renaissance buildings of Europe, St Peter's or St Paul's, and these also date from about that time.

Most Hindu worship is private. It is spent in meditation, trying to control both body and mind, and fix them on God. Or it is devotion to a personal god such as Krishna, who is adored with hymns and music of passionate intensity.

There are great popular festivals throughout the year, and these are mostly in praise of the great gods: Vishnu, Krishna, Shiva, and the mother goddess Kali. At these times temples are thronged; people wash in temple tanks, salute the image, and go in procession to holy places.

For more on Hindus, see pages 68, 106, 152.

**Three-faced divine head
near Bombay**

**South Indian
temple tank**

THREE INDIAN RELIGIONS

Most Indians are Hindus, over 300 millions. But there are a number of smaller religious groups in India: Moslems, Christians, Sikhs, Jains and Parsis. Now we shall say something about the last three together.

The Jains are followers of holy men called Jinas or 'conquerors'. Most of these lived in very ancient times, and the latest of them, Mahavira, about whom we shall hear more later, lived in the sixth century B.C. These conquerors really take the place of the Hindu gods, for it is said that even the gods have to be born again as holy men before their final salvation.

Jain worship is similar to that of the

Swastika, an ancient Indian sign used by the Jains

Hindus. Every morning men recite sacred texts as they get up, and tell prayer-beads while saluting five kinds of spiritual beings. Then they vow to live a good life, and not to injure any living being. If they have time laymen go to the temples, and there they bow before twenty-four images of the conquerors. Offerings are given to priests who place them in front of the images; usually rice is offered on a tray marked with a swastika, a sign of 'well-being' and consecration. This is a very ancient symbol (distorted by Hitler for his purposes) thousands of years old, and it was originally perhaps a representation of the sun and its rays.

The Jain temples are some of the finest in the world. For although this has always been a small religion, yet it attracted rich people. Its followers were forbidden to follow any occupation that involved taking life, so they kept mainly to trade and became rich. There are cities in north India with hundreds of Jain temples, and some have marble fretted work in decoration unequalled anywhere in the world. Other places have great statues of Jain saints cut of the solid rock on a hillside. We shall see something of Jain teachings later, but it can be noted already that they are a very peaceful people, with a strong dislike of taking life. Some of their modern temples have animal hospitals attached to them, and over the door of the temple may be an inscription, 'Non-violence is the highest religion.'

Jain stone image

The name 'Parsis' (or Parsees) means Persians, for these people came down into India from Persia from the eighth century A.D. onwards. The Moslems had occupied and ruled their land, and they wished to preserve their ancient faith intact. Today they are found chiefly in Bombay and some other cities and a few places in East Africa. Though such a small minority they are very active, educated and influential.

The founder of the Parsi religion was Zoroaster, about whom more will be said later. He lived in the sixth century B.C. and taught faith in one God, called Ahura Mazda, 'Lord Wisdom'. The old Persian gods, which were like the Hindu gods, were abolished and faith was taught in one God, the creator and one who is wholly good. To serve him truly man must live the good life and fight against all evil.

Every Parsi says an ancient prayer every morning, often repeating it on prayer-beads. It is in a very old Persian language which is hard to translate, but it teaches faith in one God, and says that the man who feeds the poor gives glory to God.

Parsi temples are not large and most of them are modern, crowded into the busy streets of Bombay. They are popularly called 'fire-temples', because inside there is a sacred fire which is always kept burning. There are no images, but there are royal symbols of crowns and swords. Parsi temples are closed to those who are not Parsis and this is one of the few religions that do not allow members of other religions to enter their holy places; it is thought that people should be content with the religion into which they were born. Parsi laymen bring gifts and sweet-smelling wood to the priests who burn it on the sacred fire. The fire is used in the worship of God, and Ahura Mazda alone is worshipped. Another prayer that is used every day says, 'Piety is the best good. Happiness comes to him who shows the best piety.'

Parsi symbol of
Ahura Mazda

Parsi Fire Temple,
Bombay

The Sikhs are the 'disciples' of Nanak, an Indian teacher who lived in the fifteenth century A.D. So the Sikh religion is one of the most recent of the world's faiths. It arose in the Punjab in north India and that is still its main centre. Sikhs are easily recognised for they always have beards and wear turbans.

The Sikh religion is a faith related to both Islam and Hinduism, and which was given special force by Nanak and his followers. From both the Sikhs learnt belief in one God, and they call him the Name (Nam). From the Hindus they took the style of their temples and some beliefs like that of rebirth after death. Because they were often persecuted, the Sikhs formed a military brotherhood, all of whose members are called 'lion' (Singh).

Sikh prayers every day begin with the memory of God, as Nanak told them: 'In the sweet hours of morning, meditate on the grace of the true Name.' Nanak and other teachers, called *gurus* (teachers), are also remembered: 'Having first remembered God almighty, think of Guru Nanak, turn your thoughts to the teaching of the scriptures, and call upon God.'

Sikh temples are often partly covered with gold leaf. Their central town is Amritsar, in the Punjab, and here there is a Golden Temple standing in the middle of an artificial lake or tank. There are no images in the temples, but the sacred book, called Granth ('book'), is read all day long in a low chant

Sikh warrior's sword and bracelet

by a succession of readers. The scripture is brought out every morning in a silver casket or ark, and carried on men's shoulders from the treasury where it has been guarded during the night, past an armed guard on to the causeway which runs out into the lake to the Golden Temple. There it is placed on a cushion under a canopy, and the readers squat behind to chant its verses. Worshippers come and stand with hands together to bow before it, and then pass round it, in clockwise direction. A communion food of sweetmeats is given to worshippers after they have placed their gifts in front of the book. In their homes Sikhs have copies of their scriptures, which they read in their own language. The scriptures teach them love and devotion to God: 'He dwells in everything; he dwells in every heart; yet he is not blended with everything; he is separated.' So from Islam the Sikh religion teaches that God is great, and from the Hindus it teaches that God is within.

For more on these religions, see pages 64, 69, 74, 112–119, 156–9.

Golden Temple of the Sikhs, Amritsar

31

BUDDHIST MEDITATION

One of the world's largest religions is Buddhism, founded by Gautama the Buddha in the sixth century B.C. It began in India but soon spread to most of the eastern parts of Asia. After more than a thousand years Buddhism died out in India, but today it is the dominant religion in South-east Asia (Ceylon, Burma, Siam, Laos and Cambodia). In China, Japan and Tibet it is one of the strongest religious forces.

Buddhism has many monks, who form the Order, especially in South-east Asia, Japan and Tibet. But the monasteries are rarely entirely closed to the outside world, and in some countries every boy spends some months or years in a monastery as part of his education. Here he learns the Teaching (*Dharma*) or Law of the Buddha, and learns to control his mind and body in meditation.

Every morning the Southern Buddhist says:

I go to the Buddha for refuge,
I go to the Teaching for refuge,
I go to the Order for refuge.

The Buddha means 'enlightened one', and Gautama the founder received full enlightenment about the mystery of life and suffering,

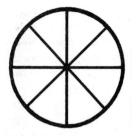

Eight-spoked Wheel, symbol of Buddha's Eightfold Way

and taught it to his followers. So they go to him for help, and try to follow his example. As with the Jains, the Hindu gods are sometimes admitted, but they are thought to be inferior to the Buddhas. In front of the statues of the Buddha the worshipper bows, kneels and even prostrates. He may pray, in times of special need. But generally he sits cross-legged, like many Buddha statues, and meditates. He thinks about his life, and confesses wrong that he may have done. He vows to give up evil: theft, lies, immorality, alcohol, and taking life. Then, with body perfectly still, he may mutter sacred texts, or try to clear his mind completely of every thought and so pass beyond the world to perfect peace and tranquillity.

Buddhist Pagoda, Ceylon

32

Amida Buddha,
giant bronze
image, Japan

In the Southern Buddhist countries there are many temples or pagodas, thin tapering buildings like pyramids. These are supposed to contain relics, teeth and hairs of past Buddhas. Worshippers cannot go into them, but in front there may be a small shrine containing images of Buddhas, and here people sit and meditate. Women as well as men go there to be quiet from the noise of city life, and to arrange their lives in the way of peace. Some pagodas are rich and famous, like the great Golden Pagoda of Rangoon, which is higher than St Paul's Cathedral and covered with gold leaf which is constantly renewed.

Worship is private and not organised. As in Hindu temples people come and go when they please, and there is no fixed service or ritual. Only occasionally are there seasonal festivals, when great crowds gather and celebrate some event in the life of the Buddha, or the beginning and end of rains. Round the open courtyards of the pagoda are many smaller shrines, with images, and also monastery rest-rooms with scriptures to read.

In China and Japan Buddhism has mixed with other religions, but its chief practice is still meditation. In these Northern Buddhist countries many other Buddhas and noble beings are believed in that are not known to the Southern Buddhists. There is Amida, the 'Buddha of Infinite Light', who calls men to rest in his Pure Land or Western Paradise. His followers call upon him every day in the words, 'Adoration to Amida'. Another noble one is Kwanyin, sometimes called 'goddess of mercy', but more accurately she is 'one who looks down in compassion'. The compassion of these holy beings, their grace to mankind and the faith that they arouse, is not only confined to prayers and meditation. Their followers are called to show the same compassion to other people, and they take vows to serve suffering humanity and not to seek their own salvation till all beings are saved.

There are many varieties of Northern Buddhism; some have become well known in the West. One called Zen takes its name from the practice of 'meditation', and although it does not use some of the holy texts that others employ, yet it stresses meditation as they do. The temples, pagodas and monasteries are like those of Southern Buddhism, though built in Chinese and Japanese style. Under Communism many Chinese temples and monasteries have been destroyed, or changed into schools and barracks. But others have been restored and their images repaired if they have historic or artistic importance.

Tibet is one of the most completely Buddhist countries, though of the Northern kind, with many Buddhas. The Dalai Lama, the spiritual ruler, is thought to be a rebirth of Kwanyin or Chenresi. Like all Northern Buddhists the Tibetans reverence a special scripture called the Lotus Scripture, and they call its teaching the Jewel. So every day the favourite prayer of Tibetans is: 'Hail to the Jewel in the Lotus.' This is repeated on prayer-beads. But there are also prayer-wheels in temples, or turning in rivers like mill wheels, and fixed as cowls on chimney-pots. There are prayer-flags, long strips of cotton with prayers and texts printed on them and fluttering from long poles. There are prayer-walls with texts on them, and people walk round them in a clockwise direction.

There are temples and pagoda-like buildings containing relics. There were great monasteries, to which many boys went. There were great services with lights and incense and bells, that have been compared with Roman Catholic services. The Chinese Communist invasion in 1959 destroyed many of the monasteries, but Buddhism remains the faith of the people of Tibet, and the Dalai Lama, though in exile in India, is still their spiritual ruler.

All Northern Buddhists vow to subdue their passions, master the teachings, save all beings, and attain to the truth of the Buddhas.

For more on Buddhism, see pages 68, 120, 161.

Tibetan wayside shrine with prayer flags

34

CHINESE AND JAPANESE WAYS

We have seen that Buddhism became one of the religions of China, but there were two others that were native to China and that partly mixed with Buddhism. One was the Way (Tao, pronounced Dow) which taught that happiness comes from following the Way of nature, the Way of heaven and the Way of earth. This entered even into Buddhism to produce the Zen sect which taught the way to peace by meditation. The Way was the most ancient and subtle teaching of China, and one which still affects her thinking. Its symbol is the circle divided into two pear-shaped halves, illustrated on this page. These two halves represent Yang and Yin. Yang is light, the sun, heaven, and the male. Yin is dark, earth and female. The universe works by the union of these two. This circle is a very common decoration, on gates, houses and cooking-pots. The pear-

Chinese symbol of
Yang and Yin

Temple of Heaven,
Peking

shaped design travelled far and wide, to India and Europe, and you may have it on your tie, scarf or carpet.

The other Chinese religious force is associated with the name of Confucius. Confucius, whose life will be described later, was a teacher of good behaviour and state laws. He was not really a teacher of religion, but he was a devout man who said, 'Heaven

begat the virtue that is in me. He who sins against heaven has nowhere left for prayer.' After his death the teachings of Confucius were adopted by the state, and for many centuries scholars trained in his way were guides to the emperors.

In the times of the Chinese empire, till the republican revolution in 1911, sacrifices were made daily and at intervals throughout the seasons to the supreme God at various altars and above all at the great Temple of Heaven in Peking. This covers an immense space, large enough for a city of 50,000 people. The emperor moved in procession from one great marble terrace to another till he reached the Altar of Heaven which is open to the sky. There the emperor prayed, beginning:

> O thou great God, thou hast assured us that thou wilt hear us, for thou carest for us as a father.

Today these services are held no more, but the Temple of Heaven is repaired and open to the public, and great public meetings are held in its grounds which are not unlike state rituals of the past.

In olden days too, the Chinese made many offerings to their dead, the ancestors. Every home had a cabinet containing wooden tablets on which were written the names of recently dead people; older tablets were put in a larger clan hall. Daily incense and prayer would be made, bowing before these tablets. Much of this remains, since people keep on dying and their families do not like to forget them. But many big ceremonies have gone, to be replaced by political gatherings. Confucius himself used to be honoured by sacrifices and festivals. Most of these have disappeared, but the teachings of Confucius remain for people to read.

It is Buddhism and the Way that are among the deepest religious forces in China. There are today official Chinese Buddhist and Taoist associations. The Way had become mixed up with a great deal of superstition and idolatry, and a reformation was overdue to get rid of much rubbish. This has been done and it has made it easier to see the real value of the ancient teachings of the Way. Many Chinese treasure these as their own ancient religious faith, they borrow books on it from libraries and have their own copies by their pillows at night. They meditate upon the profound and mysterious teachings of the Way.

Buddhism went to Japan too, and mixed with its ancient religion. The old Japanese religion had many gods, and so the Buddhists called it Shen-Tao, 'the Way of the Gods', (Shen), known as Shinto. This was to distinguish it from the Way of the Buddha (Buddha-Tao). The old Japanese gods were countless, most of them connected with nature: the sky, mountains, rivers, sea, crops and animals. The chief of them all was the sun-goddess, Amaterasu, called the Heaven-shining-august-goddess.

According to old Japanese stories Amaterasu sent her son to rule over the Japanese islands. He married the daughter of Mount Fuji, the snow-capped mountain that is seen in so many Japanese paintings. It was their grandson who became the first emperor of Japan. Other noble Japanese families claimed descent from other gods, but the emperor was first because he came from the supreme goddess. This gave rise to the idea that the emperor (the Mikado) was divine, and so he was almost worshipped in recent times, though not in olden days. But the present emperor has denied this idea and tries to rule as a constitutional monarch.

There are countless Shinto shrines, some small, others more important. But they are all made of wood and so are not very ancient. They are usually set in large areas of garden or parkland, filled with trees and streams. Both the Japanese and the Chinese have great love of nature, and their temples are often in beautiful forest or mountain places. The Shinto temple is approached through wooden or stone gateways (illustrated on right) and the worshipper goes through avenues of trees to the shrine. There he bows, claps his hands, utters texts and prayers. But there is no public worship, and priests perform rites on their own.

The most famous Shinto shrine is that of Amaterasu at Isé on the south coast. It is a very sacred spot, which every Japanese is supposed to visit once in his lifetime. There are miles of grounds, but only a simple wooden shrine which is renewed every

Gateway to Japanese Temple grounds

Japanese Buddhists have great temples and regular services to which many people go every week. For a time Buddhism almost took over Shinto and used many of its shrines, putting images in them. But after a thousand years Shinto broke away again and today its shrines are separate from the Buddhist temples and priests. The sanctuary at Isé was always kept for pure Shinto, and royal weddings and events are consecrated there. Most Japanese homes have little shelves for worship in either Buddhist or Shinto fashion, and here prayers are said and water and flowers placed every day.

twenty years. It has no images, but symbols of a mirror, sword and jewels.

For more on China and Japan, see pages 79, 126, 166.

Shinto temple, Japan

AFRICAN PRAYERS

The religions we have been learning about have histories and written scriptures. Some are purely national religions, like Hinduism and Shinto. Others are missionary, and have spread into many countries; like Christianity, Islam and Buddhism. But all have some known and recorded history, and they use written texts in their worship.

There are many other people in the world who have little or no written history of their religions, and no scriptures. This is because the art of writing is a rare thing. Most of our modern writing springs from two sources, one in the Near East, the other in China. But other countries were cut off by sea, desert or forest from the sources of writing. The ancient cultures of central and south America, Aztecs, Mayas and Incas, with strong religions, had no writing, though they built fine temples. Most of these people have now become Christians. There are other mountain and forest tribes in India or China, who are becoming Hindu or Buddhist. In Australia the aborigines, who number about 50,000, are becoming Christian.

But in Africa there are still many people

Ashanti prayer pattern

who have their old religion, but no scriptures. Many Africans have become Christians or Moslems, and these are mainly educated ones who travel abroad. But over 50 million Africans live in the forests and villages and follow the ancient religious ways of their fathers. Others who have accepted Christianity or Islam interpret these religions in their own way, and the old beliefs will linger with them for a long time.

Nearly all Africans believe in a supreme God, creator of heaven and earth and all men. The pattern at the top of this page used to hang above a door in the palace of the

African temple and
sacred tree

38

king of Ashanti in Ghana. The pattern meant, 'O God, there is something above, let it reach me.' The king would touch it and repeat these words three times. Many African sayings and proverbs speak of man's belief in God: 'If God could die, I would die', 'As the sea is never dry, so the mercy of God never ceases', 'There is no king like God.'

Like Indians and many other people of old, Africans often believe in many gods, and in the power of their dead fathers as well. Every morning many men stand in front of small shrines or images, and ask the blessing of God or one of the lesser gods upon their family and daily work. On special occasions, at ploughing and harvest, they place gifts of food at these shrines.

There are not many temples of the creator God, because people say he is too great to be kept to a temple. But in some countries of east and west Africa there are groves of trees, or small altars where gifts are placed for the great God of heaven. In other places people pour out a little water on the ground as they call upon his name. In addition to this it is often said that whenever gifts are made to the nature gods, then these gods

Pots and metal stands for sacrifices

take the heart of the sacrifice and present it to the ruler of all.

African men and women believe in God, because they see in him the creator of all men, and the one who is Providence caring for everybody. 'God looks after the tailless cow', they say. And again, 'God is the great one, whose circular head-dress is the horizon.'

For more on Africa see page 170.

CHECK YOUR READING

What is a Hindu?
What is the meaning of caste?
Recite the Mother of the Vedas.
Is an image really worshipped?
What does the three-faced image represent?
Who were the first Jains?
What is the meaning of the swastika?
Explain the meaning of non-violence.
Who are the Parsis?
What is the Parsi name for God?
Why are Parsi temples called 'fire-temples'?
Who are the Sikhs?
Where do most Sikhs live?
What is the Sikh name for God?

Who founded Buddhism?
What does the name Buddha mean?
Describe a pagoda.
Who is Kwanyin?
Where are prayer-wheels found?
What does the Yang and Yin circle represent?
Where is the Temple of Heaven?
Where were the ancestral tablets kept?
What does Shinto mean?
Who is Amaterasu?
Where are Shinto temples situated?
Do Africans believe in God?
Quote an African proverb.

Hear this call of mine: be gracious unto us this day,
Longing for help I cry to thee.
Thou, O wise God, art lord of all, thou art king of earth and heaven;
Hear, and reply with prosperity.

From the Hindu Vedas

From the unreal lead me to the real,
From darkness lead me to light.
From death lead me to immortality.

From the Hindu Upanishads

Fix thy mind on me; be devoted to me; sacrifice to me;
Prostrate thyself before me; so shalt thou come to me.
I promise thee truly, for thou art dear to me.

From the Hindu Gita

We praise the Lord, who was the first king, the first ascetic, the first
    head of a congregation.
May there be good fortune from holy Mahavira's eyes, whose pupils
    are wide with compassion even for sinful people, moist with a
    trace of tears.

From Jain scriptures

He who knows what is bad for himself knows what is bad for others,
    and he who knows what is bad for others knows what is bad for
    himself. This interchange should always be borne in mind.
Those whose minds are at peace and who are free from passions do
    not desire to live at the expense of others.

From Jain scriptures

With hands outstretched in prayer for support
I will ask first of all, O Wise One with Righteousness,
The acts of the Holy Spirit,
To satisfy the will of the Good Mind.

To me who would worship you, O Wise Lord with the Good Mind,
According to Righteousness give success in both worlds,
— That of body and that of mind —
To support me through them and bring me to bliss.

Prayers of Zoroaster

There is but one God, whose name is True, the Creator, devoid of
    fear and enmity,
    immortal, unborn, self-existent, great and bountiful;
The True One was in the beginning, the True One was in the primal age.
The True One is, was, and the True One shall also be.

Sikh morning prayer

God has his seat everywhere, his treasure houses are in all places.
Whatever a man's portion is, God at the creation apportioned him
    that.share once and for all.
Hail, all hail unto him, let your greetings be to the Primal Lord;
Pure and without beginning, changeless, the same from age to age.

Sikh prayer by Nanak

Hindus bathing in the Ganges

Just as an arrow-maker makes straight his arrow, the wise man makes
    straight his trembling, unsteady thought which is difficult to guard
    and difficult to restrain.
Let the wise man guard his thought, which is difficult to perceive,
    which is extremely subtle, which wanders at will.
Thought which is well guarded is the bearer of happiness.

From the Buddhist Way of Virtue

41

Thou perfect master, who shinest upon all things and all men,
As gleaming moonlight plays upon a thousand waters at the same time,
Thy great compassion does not pass by a single creature.
Steadily and quietly sails the great ship of compassion across the sea
of sorrow.
Thou art the great physician for a sick and impure world,
In pity giving invitation to the Paradise of the West.

Chinese Buddhist verse

The man who at the sight of gain remembers justice,
Who when he sees danger is ready to give up his destiny,
And who never forgets an old agreement —
Such a one must be counted a perfect man.

Saying of Confucius

God Most High — how he is majestic!
In his world governance exalted and mighty!
He reaches out to all places of the world,
To give confidence to peoples, and create order.

Late Confucian ode

The highest good is like that of water.
The goodness of water is that it benefits ten thousand creatures; yet
itself does not scramble, but is content with the places that all men
disdain.
It is this that makes water so near to the Way.

Wealth and place breed insolence
That brings ruin in its train.
When your work is done, then withdraw.
Such is Heaven's Way.

From the Chinese Way

If you want to know, come unto me and I will explain to you the origin
of all things.
I, God the Parent, reveal myself and I will explain to you everything
in detail; then the whole world will rejoice.
I hasten to save the world; therefore you people in the world exult.

Modern Shinto song

The stream crosses the path, the path crosses the stream,
Which of them is the elder?
Did we not cut a path long ago to go and meet this stream?
The stream had its origin long, long ago.
The stream had its origin in the Creator.
He created things,
Pure, pure Tano.

Ashanti song

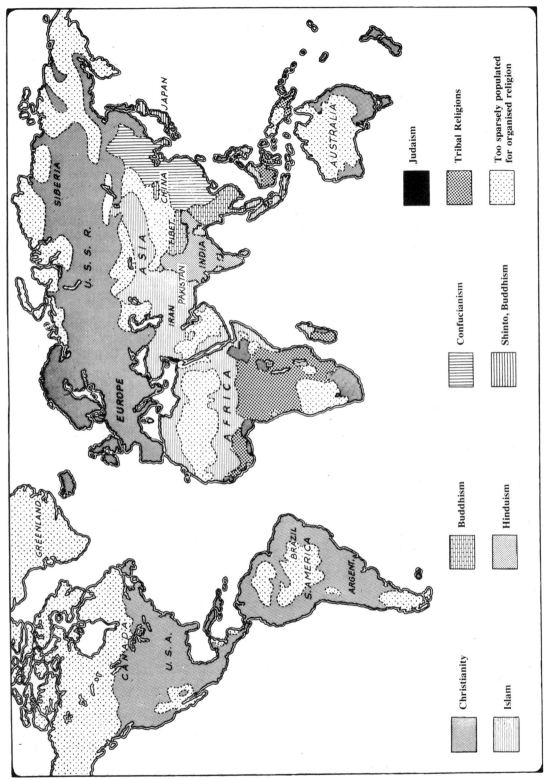

WORLD RELIGIONS

Christianity

Islam

Buddhism

Hinduism

Confucianism

Shinto, Buddhism

Judaism

Tribal Religions

Too sparsely populated
for organised religion

43

THE STORY OF RELIGION

Nobody knows when religion began, but it is likely that in some form it is almost as old as the human race itself. When thinking man, modern man, first emerged it was not long before he began to puzzle over the problems of life and death and the universe. We have evidence of this from the Old Stone Age, about 20,000 years ago, and it probably goes much farther back.

From the Old Stone Age onwards there have survived stone statues, earthenware pots, bones of the dead, paintings, ruins of altars and holy places, all of which show that different kinds of religion were practised. But before this time there is hardly any

evidence. It is the same for the history of civilisation in general, for social and political groupings. There are hardly any remains, so it is difficult to form a picture of the earliest days.

It used to be thought that we could guess what the earliest prehistoric men did and thought, by studying so-called 'primitive' people today, in Australia, South America, or the forest pygmies in Africa. These people may have a low standard of religion, yet that does not mean that their religion is simple. And although they have no written history, yet they are not 'prehistoric' in the sense that their practices are the same as those of their

Stonehenge

44

**Prehistoric deer and bull
cave-painting, France**

forefathers thousands of years ago. They too have a history, though unwritten.

The idea of evolution, growth in culture, shows how beliefs and practices can be purified and can develop. But also history shows us examples of decline or 'devolution', and many mixtures of high and low ideas together. We could speak of the development of religion from magic to belief in spirits, to belief in many gods, and at last to belief in one God. But many quite 'primitive' people believe in a supreme God, creator of the world, high above all the rest.

In the painted caves of south-west France and northern Spain there are splendid examples of the magic art from 13,000 B.C.

Old Stone Age men painted on the walls inside dark caves, at Lascaux and elsewhere, pictures of the animals they wanted to kill in hunting. This shows that they were clever artists, almost as good as some modern artists, for the animals are pictured in fine detail and action. But very rarely are men shown in pictures, and then in crude outline. This was not because the artists could not paint men, but they were not usually interested in doing it for magic ritual.

In other places there are statues; small stone ones have survived, mostly of mother figures. These show a concern with the growth of the family, but there are rarely any male figures. Some writers think that

**Mummy, and soul like a bird,
from an Egyptian painting**

these ancient people believed in a Mother Goddess, creator of children who was also identified with the Earth and the growth of the crops. It seems likely that they also believed in a God of the sky, creator of the world. But they did not make images of him, for how could they make images of the sky? They probably believed in other spirits, of hills and trees, stones and rivers, as men did later on. But again they left little trace of belief in such things.

From very early times men were troubled by the fact of death. In the Old Stone Age, and before, men often buried the dead in a way that suggested they believed in a life

after death. The bones are put in a curled up position, like an unborn baby. The skull or other bones are painted red like blood. Pots and weapons are put by the body, showing that they were to be used in the 'happy hunting grounds' after death.

All these ideas and many more are seen clearly in the more abundant remains that we have of the New Stone Age, about 7,000 years ago. These are seen in the 'Fertile Crescent', that stretches from Egypt, up through Palestine and Syria, and across to Mesopotamia or Iraq. But it goes beyond this into Persia and north-west India. Here began civilisation as we know it. In Egypt,

The Ziggurat
at Ur, Iraq

in particular, there was great concern with life after death, and eventually the pyramids were built to house the bodies which were embalmed or preserved to give an appearance of immortality. In many of the world's great museums there are bodies from Egypt with the skin still intact, which go back 5,000 and 6,000 years. The Egyptians performed a ceremony of 'opening the mouth' of a body to re-create a 'living soul', and give it strength to meet any dangers in the next life.

In Mesopotamia great temples (*ziggurats*) were built with steps up them, like the Tower of Babel in the Bible, which by seeming to reach nearly up to heaven brought man nearer to the gods.

In India, great temple baths or tanks were built, in which people washed themselves to purify body and soul for the service of the gods. Similar tanks are found at most Indian temples today.

From Mesopotamia came the Jewish or Hebrew people, wandering across the Fertile Crescent to Egypt, and finally settling down in Palestine between these two great centres of civilisation, and always being astride the roads that connected them. After their Exodus or 'coming out' of Egypt the Hebrews made a covenant or agreement

47

with God, and this gave their religion a historical beginning. In their later struggles as a nation they came to think of the importance of their history even more. They saw themselves as a Chosen People, selected by God to 'give light to the Gentiles'. Other nations round about, Egyptians, Syrians and so on, all had their religions. But it was the Hebrew religion alone that survived. It was reformed and purified by priests and prophets, and it remains to this day.

The Hebrews and neighbouring peoples claimed to be descended from Shem, one of the sons of Noah after the Flood. So they are called Semites, 'descendants of Shem', though this term is not fully accurate. From the Hebrew inspiration came other religions that are also called Semitic: Christianity and Islam. Christianity arose from among the Jews, in Palestine, but soon spread outside the Hebrew world into Europe, north Africa, and parts of Asia. Islam arose in Arabia, among people related to the Hebrews though different from them. Many Moslem ideas are similar to those of the Hebrews and Christians. But in time Islam spread far beyond Arabia and the Semitic world, into Africa, Asia, and even Europe.

The three Semitic religions are one great branch of the religious development of mankind. But there is another great branch, just as important, and that is the Indian. Mesopotamia and Persia were once similar in religion to India, but eventually they became Moslem and remain so now. India is a great fountain of religious thought that has spread in different forms to the most easterly parts of Asia.

Indian religion began with the ancient cities in the valley of the river Indus, with their temple tanks (see page 152). These were destroyed by invaders from the north, Aryans, who came into India about the time of the Hebrew Exodus from Egypt, around 1500 B.C. The religion of the invaders gradually mixed with that of the Indus people, and produced finally what we call Hinduism. This religion has had many great sages and holy books.

The sixth and fifth centuries B.C. were wonderful times in religion, the Golden Age. In Palestine the prophets Jeremiah, Ezekiel and a later Isaiah were teaching. In Greece the first thinkers, Pythagoras and Thales were doing their work. In Persia was the prophet Zoroaster. In India were Gautama Buddha and Mahavira of the Jains, in China Confucius and Lao Tse.

The Buddha and Mahavira were only two of many teachers in India at this time, but they broke away from Hinduism to take their ideas beyond. Buddhism eventually spread to Ceylon and Burma, and then to China, Tibet and Japan by the sixth century A.D.

Zoroaster of Persia stands just about midway between the Hebrew and the Indian branches of religion. He taught belief in one God, yet that God's name resembles some of the Indian names.

Confucius and Lao Tse, and the Japanese Shinto religion, also were religious growths that developed on their own for centuries. But we have already seen how Buddhism came with Indian ideas to mingle with these native Chinese and Japanese faiths. And so finally Indian ideas came to be as influential on the Far East as Hebrew ideas have been upon the Far West.

For many centuries the Semitic and the Indian religions lived apart, hardly knowing anything about each other. Christian missions went to India in the early centuries, but in small numbers. Some Buddhists came West, but their influence was not lasting. Islam later went to India in strength. There was some mingling with Hindu religion and, as we have seen, the Sikh religion arose from such a mingling. But in the main Hindus and Moslems lived apart.

Only today are the religions of the world fully in contact with one another, thanks to the easy communications of the twentieth century. Now we can learn about each other's religion. We can see where their ideas are like our own. We can notice where they are different, sometimes very different.

48

BRANCHES OF RELIGION

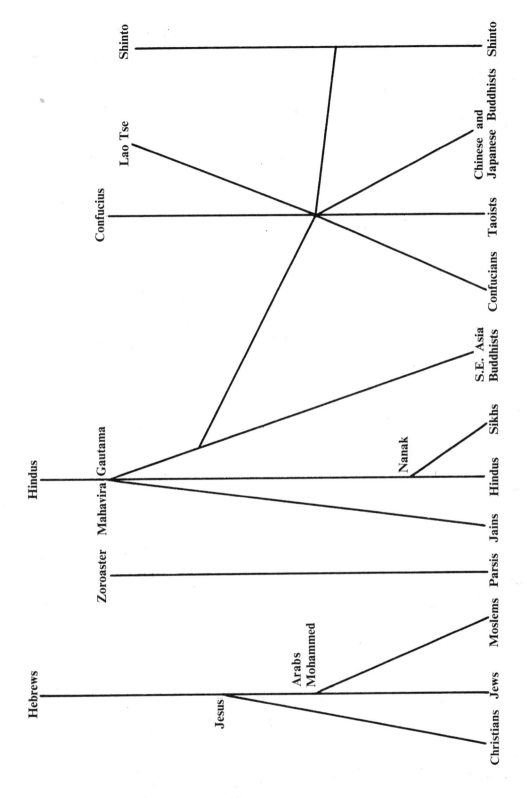

49

Part 2

THE FOUNDERS

Religions did not just grow by a simple process of evolution. Their progress depended upon the emergence of geniuses, who were so much above the level of general religious life that they had to make a new start. Without them religion and culture might languish in stagnation for centuries.

One of the most remarkable examples is Mohammed. For centuries the Arab people had lived near ancient civilisations, just outside the Fertile Crescent. Great religions had risen and fallen, or spread to far distant places, such as those of Egypt and Babylon, or Judaism and Christianity. Yet Arabia remained largely untouched. Of course much of it was desert, population was scanty and trade routes few. But the Arab religion had not developed on its own. It had to await the coming of a great man, Mohammed, in the seventh century A.D., before it sprang to life and became so powerful that it burst out of Arabia and spread to the farthest limits of the known world. More than most religions Islam is the creation of one man.

In some other religions there is much less

stress upon a founder. This is particularly true in India. We saw that the Jews gave great importance to history, and they regarded their religion as due to the way God led their nation down its long history. In India history was not thought to be of such importance; at any rate history was not written in the same way. So in the Hindu religion there is only sketchy history and no real founder. But this does not mean that there were no outstanding thinkers who helped the religion on and developed its teachings. There have been long lines of these in fact all down Hindu life and practice.

Many founders, perhaps all, have also been reformers. This means that they did not start from nothing and just think up a religion on their own. They were never isolated, but were helped by groups of other thinkers and disciples. They grew up in a religious environment, for we have seen that religion is as old as mankind. They inherited ideas from their predecessors. They accepted some and developed them. Others they rejected as outworn or even false. Confucius was not a religious founder, but he was a reformer who tried to order both society and religious ritual according to the best principles.

In the following pages we shall find short biographies of the chief founders of the religions of the world. We shall start with those of the Semitic tradition, Moses, Jesus and Mohammed. Then we shall pass to Zoroaster of Persia, and the Indian sages, including Mahavira, Gautama and Nanak. Finally we shall come to the Chinese. With the Japanese, as with African and other religions, the early history is obscure, and it is difficult to trace out the founders. There are some legends of great prophets or priests, but these are very vague. And in a great continent like Africa, where there was no central state or organization, there were countless priests and no common religion. Only today is some of the history being pieced out, and then in fragments. The same was true of ancient Europe and America. So it is to Asia that we turn, for Asia is the home of every religion that has lasted down the centuries.

MOSES

This book began with a description of Moslems at prayer. This was done so as to interest Christian and Jewish readers in other religions, and because Moslem worship is new to them. But we learned that the religion of the Moslems arose later than that of the Jews, and so now we shall go back to the historical order and speak of the Hebrews first.

The word Hebrews is used for all the tribes in the early Bible story. They were later called Israelites after Jacob, whose name was also Israel. The word Jew comes from the later tribe of Judah. It is used after the other tribes had been carried away to exile in the eighth century B.C., leaving only Judah, and especially for the time after the Exile of Judah in the fifth century, or even as late as the beginning of the Christian era. Today we speak of Jews. We call their forefathers Hebrews.

We have seen that the Hebrew branch of religion is one of the oldest, along with the Hindus. It really begins with Moses. Before him there had been the Patriarchs, the 'fathers': Abraham, Isaac and Jacob. Somewhere about 2000 B.C. Abraham left Ur in Mesopotamia, and travelled down the Fertile Crescent to what was later called Palestine (after the Philistine invaders). Abraham and his sons worshipped God under various names, of which the chief was Elohim, simply meaning God. Jacob and his twelve sons, founders of the twelve tribes of Israel (Jacob's new name) went down into Egypt because of famine. There they were enslaved and made to work building store cities. It was Moses who led them out again and made them a nation, about 1300 or 1200 B.C.

Moses was one of the most remarkable men of history. His name was Egyptian, and

Great
Pyramid
and
Sphinx

52

the stories told about his birth and preservation are similar to others about great people of old. While in flight from Egypt he married the daughter of a priest Jethro and had a revelation of God on Mount Sinai. Sinai seems to have been volcanic, and this is suggested by the story of the 'burning bush'. But it was the call from God that was important. God revealed himself to Moses under a new name, 'I am that I am.' This seems to mean both that God is the living one, and that he is mysterious: no man can fully understand him. The name is represented in the Bible by four consonants YHWH, usually translated in English as Jehovah, but the vowels are probably incorrect. It is written in capitals as LORD in English Bibles.

God told Moses to return to Egypt to bring out his people, and they would come to worship him at Mount Sinai. Moses did this, taking with him his brother Aaron as spokesman. The Pharaoh or king of Egypt was unwilling to let these good slaves go,

but after 'plagues' of floods, locusts and disease the Israelites escaped. The Passover was celebrated because they had been 'passed over' in the plagues, and it is still kept today.

The Israelites crossed the marshes at the north end of the Red Sea, where the waters had been driven back by 'a strong east wind all the night'. Ever after, down their long history, the Hebrews remembered how God had saved them 'by a strong right hand and an outstretched arm'.

Then Moses led them to Mount Sinai. There a covenant was made between God and the people. A covenant writing was read out, a sacrifice was made, and half the blood was sprinkled on an altar for God and half over the people (Exodus 24: 6–8). The Ten Commandments were engraved on stone tablets by Moses (Exodus 34: 28). These were laws of religion and behaviour, the first four telling men's duty to God, the last six their duty to other people. The stone tablets were put in an Ark and carried about

53

by the Hebrews in their journeyings, eventually coming to rest in the temple later built by Solomon in Jerusalem. The Ark seems to have disappeared finally at the time of the Exile in the sixth century B.C.

The task of Moses was to weld the various tribes into a nation and this took years. The stay in the desert had this purpose, and only when they had been made into a powerful force were they able to invade Palestine and gradually settle there. This was done under Joshua, for Moses died in the desert. The story of Joshua, the Judges and the Kings is too long for us to deal with here. It is told in the Bible.

Moses also made Israel accept the task of being a Chosen People. Jehovah became the God of Israel, protecting them in their journeyings. Israel became the people of God, on condition that they served him faithfully. The great prophets later insisted that Israel was not chosen for her own benefit, but so that she might give light to other people, and if she failed in that she had been unfaithful to the covenant.

Later ages thought that Moses not only gave the Law, but also wrote the first five books of the Bible (Torah, or Pentateuch). The Bible itself does not say that Moses wrote all this; the titles of the books were added on later, and the book of Deuteronomy tells the story of Moses's death, which he could not have written himself. But there is no reason to doubt that Moses gave the substance of the Law, the Ten Commandments and the Book of the Covenant (Exodus 24). Here he tried to raise the level not only of religious life, but also of moral behaviour. He established family elders or judges to help him and he forbade cruel and immoral ways. Over the centuries scribes and prophets edited the Law and later writings, and the moral teachings of Israel were very high. It is here that we read the great saying, 'thou shalt love thy neighbour as thyself' (Leviticus 19:18).

Moses left an indelible mark on the Hebrews, and they said of him; 'there has not arisen a prophet since in Israel like unto Moses' (Deuteronomy 34:10). Still to this day the Jews confess in a list of articles of faith, 'I believe that the prophecy of Moses was true, and that he was the chief of the prophets.'

The Jewish Law

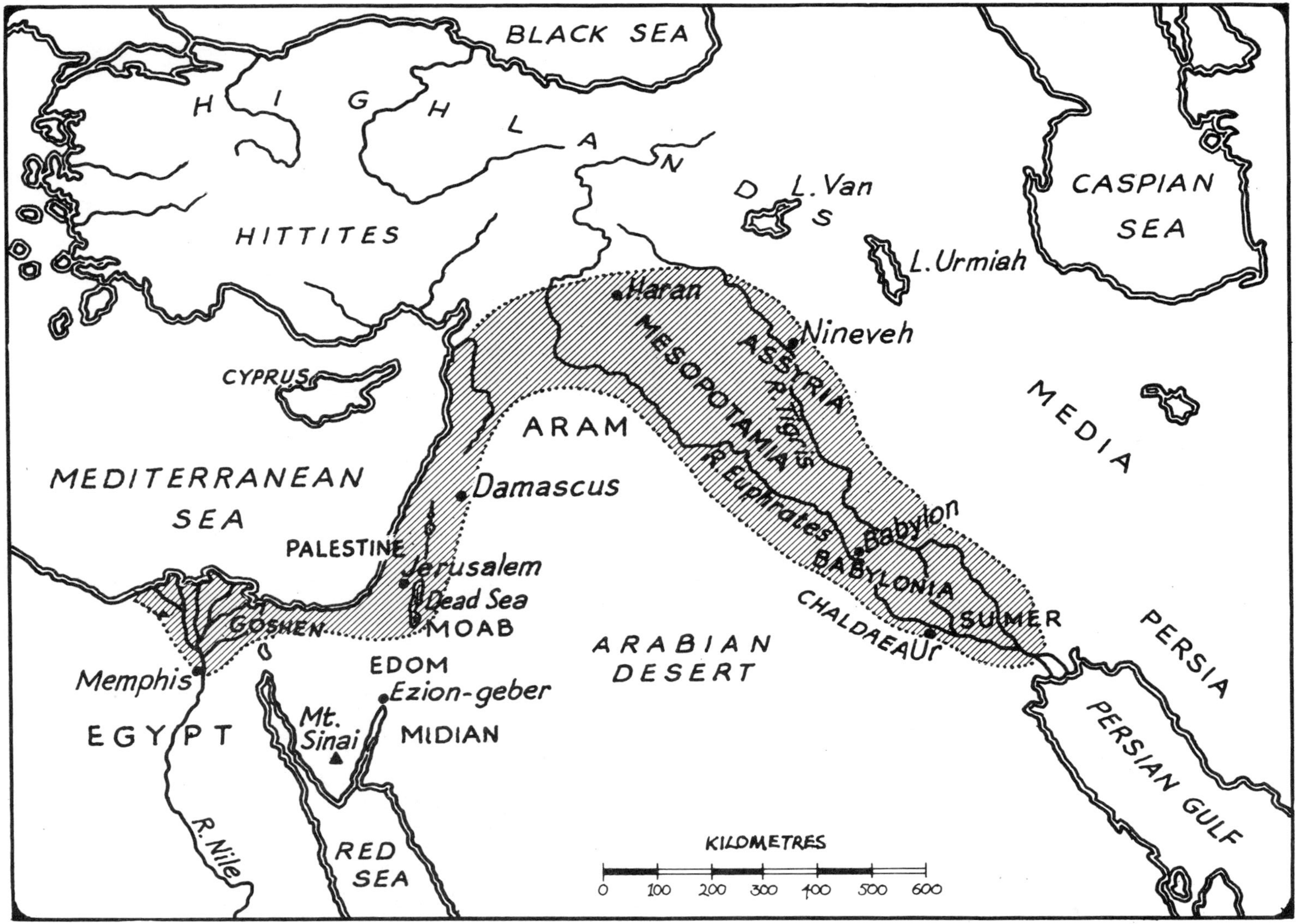

THE FERTILE CRESCENT

BLACK SEA

CASPIAN SEA

MEDITERRANEAN SEA

RED SEA

PERSIAN GULF

HITTITES

HIGHLANDS

CYPRUS

MEDIA

PERSIA

ASSYRIA

MESOPOTAMIA

Nineveh

Haran

L. Van

L. Urmiah

R. Tigris

R. Euphrates

Babylon

BABYLONIA

SUMER

CHALDAEA

ARAM

Damascus

PALESTINE

Jerusalem

Dead Sea

MOAB

EDOM

GOSHEN

Memphis

EGYPT

R. Nile

Mt. Sinai

Ezion-geber

MIDIAN

ARABIAN DESERT

KILOMETRES

0   100   200   300   400   500   600

JESUS

Jesus came after many Hebrew prophets had continued and enlarged the teaching of Moses, about love to God and love to man. He built upon the foundation of their teaching, which is why Christians include the Jewish Bible in their own Bible with its new teachings.

Jesus was a Jew, who lived all his life in Palestine. He spoke Aramaic, a language similar to the old Hebrew tongue which had passed out of popular use but was still used for reading the scriptures. Many Jews also spoke Greek which was the common language in the Roman Empire, as English is today in many parts of the world. The name of Jesus that we use is the Greek form of the Hebrew Joshua, meaning 'Saviour'.

The life and teaching of Jesus is given in the Gospel, the 'Good News'. The first three Gospels are closely similar, each one giving additional details, while the fourth, John, adds much interpretation. Two of the Gospels, Matthew and Luke, give popular stories of the birth of Jesus, which are read again every Christmas. Mary and Joseph, parents of Jesus, were already engaged to be married when they had visions and dreams of angels who told them that the son that would be born to them would be the Son of God, the hoped-for Messiah. Jesus was born in Bethlehem in the time of King Herod the Great, and wise men or star-gazers, perhaps Zoroastrians from Persia, came to pay reverence to him. Jesus was brought up in Nazareth, his parents' home town in Galilee. Later stories gave many miracles to his childhood, but the Gospels show him as a perfectly normal boy. The one story of his visit to Jerusalem shows him asking questions of the teachers in the temple, such as an intelligent boy might ask in the year before he was to be admitted to read the synagogue lessons (as we saw when talking about Jewish worship, page 18).

Galilee was a northern province of Palestine, under a succession of Jewish rulers who had to pay tribute to the Roman overlords. It was a land of mixed population, and more open to the influences of the Greek and Roman world than the more narrowly Jewish circles of Jerusalem. So the Christian religion spread more easily from here later on, into the outside world, helped on especially by the apostle Paul who came from Tarsus even further away in Asia Minor.

The Jews were hoping for a Messiah, the 'anointed one' of God ('Christ' in Greek), who would deliver them from foreign rule and set up a Kingdom or Reign of God, ruled according to the laws of God. Two centuries earlier some Jewish heroes, the Maccabees, had done this in throwing off Greek rule, but their successors had become tyrants, and were finally defeated by the Romans.

About A.D. 26 or 27 John the Baptist appeared, saying that the Kingdom of God was near, and telling people to repent and have their sins washed away by baptism in the river Jordan. He was soon arrested and executed. Jesus had already been baptised by John, and he now took up his work, and went preaching into the lakeside towns of Galilee, saying, 'the Kingdom of God is at hand, repent, and believe the Good News.'

Jesus was a different sort of man from John, less fierce, and a great story-teller, putting his teaching into homely parables which ordinary people could understand. Unlike many other religious teachers Jesus did not seek his audience only in the synagogues or among people interested in arguing about religion. He made friends with the outcasts, men and women who led bad lives, telling them that God forgave them and wanted them too in his kingdom.

56

Then again Jesus had the gift of healing. There were few doctors in those days and they knew little about the causes and cures of sickness. Jesus healed the lame and paralysed, and those who we should say suffered from delusions, thinking themselves inhabited by evil spirits. Only with the growth of modern psychology can we now understand the power of mind over body. Jesus healed both mind and body and so brought these sick people too into God's kingdom.

The idea that Jesus had of the Kingdom of God was not a political revolution against Rome by armed warfare, though some of his followers, perhaps Judas, may have hoped for that. Jesus meant rather the Reign of God over men's lives, and he said, 'the kingdom of God is within you', already in your midst. Men were quick to call him the Messiah (Christ). But his own name for himself was 'Son of Man'. This mysterious title perhaps meant that he had been chosen by God as leader of the Kingdom which a Bible verse had spoken of as being human, like a Son of Man (Daniel 7:13–18).

After two or three years of success in Galilee, and having chosen twelve disciples to extend his work, Jesus went to Jerusalem, the capital city, to challenge the Jewish religious leaders to accept the Reign of God. Here he was betrayed, accused of being a political revolutionary, and crucified by the Roman governor, Pontius Pilate. His enemies said in sarcasm, but it was truer than they knew, 'he saved others, he cannot save himself.' For Jesus had saved many from shame and disease, never thinking of himself, and giving himself to save all men.

The Sea of Galilee

57

To his disciples the crucifixion was utter disaster: how could Jesus be the Christ if God had abandoned him? But within a few days they had visions which convinced them that he had risen from the dead. The Gospels record nine appearances of Jesus to the disciples, some in Jerusalem, but chiefly in Galilee. Fifty days later, at the Jewish feast of Pentecost, the disciples were filled with the Spirit of God, and went out boldly to proclaim that 'God has made him both Lord and Christ, this Jesus whom you crucified.' The Christian church began then and spread over the world.

The teaching of Jesus is in the Gospels and it is a perfection of moral and religious teaching. 'No man ever spoke like this man', said his followers. His Sermon on the Mount (Matthew 5–7) is widely regarded as supreme. But it is not just moral teaching, about good behaviour. It is deeply religious teaching, about trust in God, and forgiving men because God forgives us.

To Christians Jesus is not just a teacher: he is the Christ, the Word of God, the Lord. He reveals the love of God to man which saves him body and soul, still today as in the first century. Jesus is not simply a past hero; he said, 'I am with you always, even to the end.'

The Church of Sacré Cœur, Paris

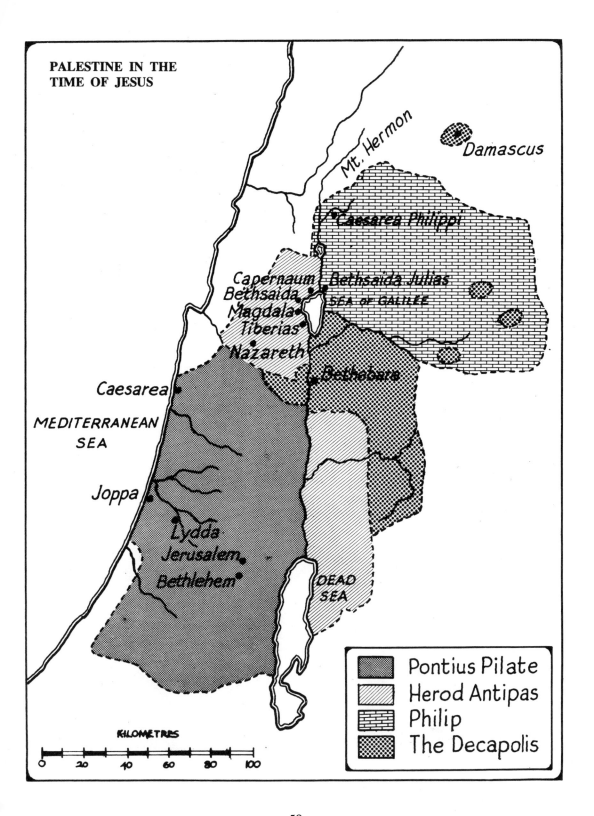

PALESTINE IN THE
TIME OF JESUS

Mt. Hermon

Damascus

Caesarea Philippi

Capernaum
Bethsaida
Magdala
Tiberias
Nazareth

Bethsaida Julias

SEA OF GALILEE

Caesarea

MEDITERRANEAN
SEA

Bethabara

Joppa

Lydda
Jerusalem
Bethlehem

DEAD
SEA

KILOMETRES

0   20   40   60   80   100

	Pontius Pilate
	Herod Antipas
	Philip
	The Decapolis

MOHAMMED

Mohammed was an Arab, born in Mecca in about the middle of western Arabia. He was born in A.D. 570, 'the year of the elephant', so called because an army from Abyssinia advanced then on Mecca, but it was defeated and its elephant was killed.

Mecca was a trading centre, where caravans stopped on their way down from Syria to the Yemen and on to India. It was also a holy place. In the centre of the city of Mecca stood a building called the Kaaba (meaning 'cube'). It was a cube-shaped building, with a flat top. In the wall of the Kaaba was fixed a Black Stone, probably a meteorite that had fallen here from the sky at some past time, and which the Arabs had taken as sent from God. So people from all over Arabia came to visit the Kaaba and kiss the Black Stone. There was also a holy well, Zamzam (so called from the noise the oozing waters made), in the courtyard near the Kaaba.

There are some legends about the birth and childhood of Mohammed. His mother is said to have had a vision of the castles of Syria, hundreds of miles away, and to have heard an angelic voice saying that she was to be the mother of the prophet of that people. And in his childhood two angels are said to have taken a clot of sin out of the child's body. But an early biographer when telling stories like this says, 'it is said, but God alone knows whether it is true.'

Mohammed's father was called Abdullah and his mother Amina. His father died

The Kaaba at Mecca

60

before the child was born, and his mother when he was six years old. He was left in the care of his grandfather, who died when Mohammed was eight. This sad childhood probably made the boy thoughtful. Although his family was not rich, and the uncle to whom he was now confided had many other cares, yet they were connected with the Kaaba. Mohammed would see pilgrims come there, and he grew to dislike the many idols that disfigured the Kaaba.

Mohammed joined in trade, the chief occupation of Mecca. When he was 25 he worked for a rich widow, Khadija, and he soon married her. Khadija was a great help to him, both in trade and in his later prophetic work. They had seven children, and while she lived Mohammed took no other wife.

When he was 40 Mohammed began to have visions. He loved solitude, and would go out into the desert and the hills to be alone for prayer and thought. One day the angel Gabriel appeared to him as a huge figure astride the horizon. Gabriel told him that he, Mohammed, was the prophet of God. He told him to recite from a book which he held out. Mohammed could not read, yet he began to recite it. This and later revelations formed the Koran, the 'recitation', the word of God for the Arab people.

Mohammed began to preach belief in one God, and he denounced the many gods and their idols. His wife Khadija believed in him; so did his servant Zaid, his cousin Ali, and then a notable man Abu Bakr. These were later his chief followers and successors. But other people despised and then persecuted them, and some followers had to flee to Christian Abyssinia for protection. In A.D. 622 Mohammed decided to migrate to the town of Medina, 200 miles to the north. The people of Medina invited him, and a number had been converted to his religion. This 'migration' is the Hegira (or Hijra) and Mohammedan dates are reckoned from there.

At Medina there were several groups of Jews and at first Mohammed hoped they would support him, and believe in his message, for he too believed in one God, in his prophets in the Bible, and in the Judgement. But the Jews did not accept him and Mohammed came to suspect them of treachery. Some he expelled, and others were executed.

At Medina Mohammed took the fateful decision to fight for his faith, by a 'holy war' (jihad). His followers were badly off and he decided to attack a Meccan caravan which was passing nearby. The Meccans sent out an army quickly, but Mohammed with 300 men defeated the Meccans with 900. The latter then sent a much larger army, and Mohammed's men suffered severely but Medina was not taken. From then on his success began. He gradually brought all the tribes of Arabia into alliances. When he felt strong enough he marched on Mecca, and in 630 the city submitted to him with hardly a struggle.

When all was quiet, and his great army in full possession, Mohammed rode into Mecca and round the Kaaba. He had all the images and paintings destroyed, except, it is said, a picture of Jesus and Mary. He called the people to prayer, in the name of God. He told them to be just in their dealings, not to avenge themselves, and to give up idolatry. Then he returned to his house in Medina.

Mohammed believed himself to be in the true succession of the great Hebrew prophets. He always spoke of Jesus with reverence, though he seems not to have understood the crucifixion, yet believed in the Resurrection or Ascension. There were not many Christians in Arabia, just a few Abyssinian slaves, and some solitary monks. It is said that in Mecca there were two Abyssinians who used to recite the Law and the Gospel, and Mohammed would listen to them. There were numerous Jews, and there is more narrative like that of the Old Testament in the Koran than of the New Testament.

Mohammed believed that as Moses had brought the Law to the Jews, and Jesus the Gospel to the Christians, so God had sent him to bring the Koran to the Arabs. He used the Arab name Allah, but it means 'God'. He had the genius to adapt the Kaaba and the Black Stone to the worship of God, and to this day the Moslem pilgrim to Mecca kisses the Black Stone and calls on God.

Mohammed had nine wives. Like Henry VIII he wanted a son to succeed him, but he was even less fortunate and no son survived him. Like David in the Bible he was a warrior, and a man of many wives, and yet a devout man of God. In 632 Mohammed died, suddenly, of intestinal trouble. His friend Abu Bakr succeeded him, and became first Caliph, 'successor' or 'deputy'.

Abu Bakr said, 'Mohammed was a man, Mohammed is dead. God is alive, immortal.' But to his followers Mohammed is the last and greatest prophet, 'the Seal of the Prophets'; sinless and intercessor between God and man.

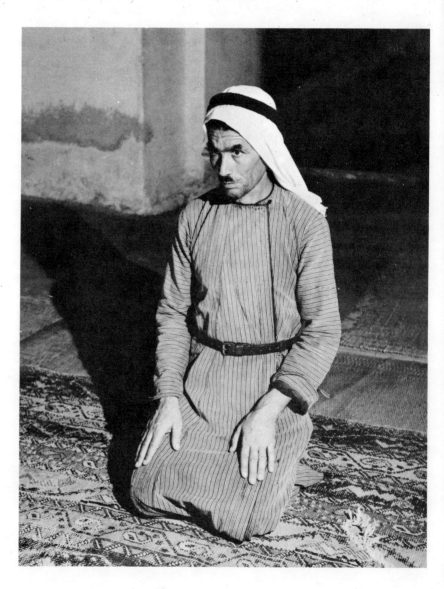

A Moslem
at prayer

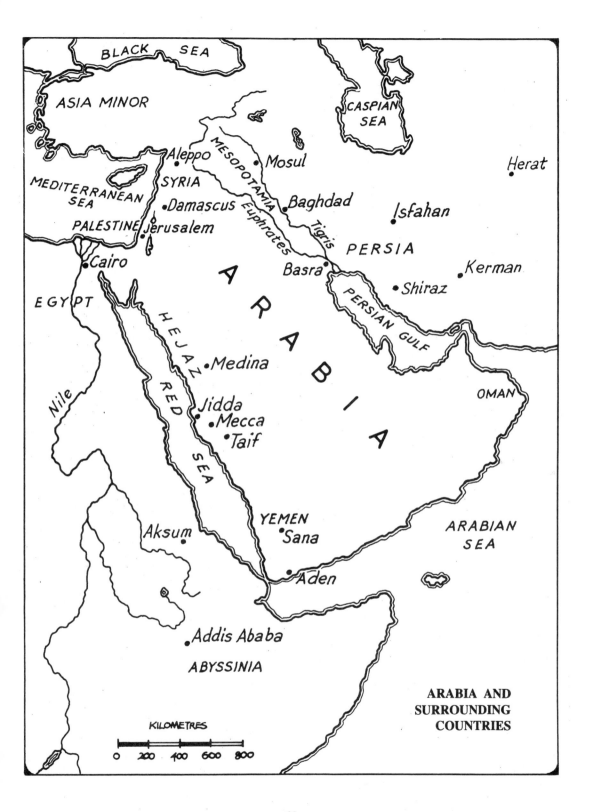

BLACK SEA

ASIA MINOR

CASPIAN SEA

MEDITERRANEAN SEA

Aleppo

SYRIA

MESOPOTAMIA

Mosul

Herat

Damascus

Baghdad

Isfahan

PALESTINE Jerusalem

Euphrates

Tigris

PERSIA

Cairo

EGYPT

A
R
A
B
I
A

Basra

Kerman

Shiraz

PERSIAN GULF

HEJAZ

Medina

Nile

RED SEA

Jidda
Mecca
Taif

OMAN

Aksum

YEMEN
Sana

ARABIAN SEA

Aden

Addis Ababa

ABYSSINIA

KILOMETRES

0   200   400   600   800

**ARABIA AND
SURROUNDING
COUNTRIES**

ZOROASTER

Zoroaster stands midway between the Hebrews and the Indians, and the religion which he founded or reformed holds to belief in one God, whom the Parsis today worship in their 'fire-temples'.

The life of Zoroaster is much less clear than that of Mohammed, and there is a good deal of legend hiding facts. But in the earliest scriptures there is seen a prophet with a deep faith in God.

The dates usually given for his life are 630–553 B.C., though these have been much disputed. His very name may be a title. In any case Zoroaster is the Greek form of Zarathushtra which is the Persian. His family name was Spitama. He lived not long before the Persian kings Cyrus and Darius, who are known in the Bible for conquering Persia and then Babylon and Palestine.

Legend says that the child glowed with heavenly light, the infant laughed at birth, and the whole of nature smiled in sympathy, while the evil spirit rushed howling to the end of the earth.

Persia had many gods, whose names were like those of India; Mithra and others. Ahura Mazda, 'Lord Wisdom', became more and more important, and was the God to whom king Darius attributed his victories. Opposed to the good God was the evil spirit, Ahriman, and it was for men to help the good and fight the evil.

For many years Zoroaster thought about God and his kingdom on earth. He wandered in desert places seeking to speak to God. At last he had a vision of the Good Mind (Vohu Mana) who led him into the presence of God. Here he was charged to tell men to worship Ahura Mazda alone and to serve him by good lives. Zoroaster was tempted by the evil Ahriman, who tried to hold him back from his mission, but he repelled the

Pillar to Ahura Mazda

64

evil one by quoting holy texts to him.

Then he spent years trying to persuade people to accept his message but without success. He was called a heretic and a sorcerer, and he wandered from place to place trying to make one convert. He did convert his cousin, but nobody else. After ten years he travelled to Bactria in the east of Persia, and here the king Vishtaspa accepted the prophet's message. This was the beginning of success, and missions are said to have been sent abroad as far as India.

After some years religious opposition broke out again, perhaps from priests who were jealous of Zoroaster's growing influence. The prophet himself was killed by the sword as he was offering the sacred fire in a temple. He died before the great success of his religion, which later became that of all Persia, and lasted till the Moslem invasion forced the remaining Parsis down into India. Still to them Zoroaster is the most holy one, who gave 'the holy faith which is of all things best'.

Carved stone head of Zoroaster

CHECK YOUR READING

Whose name was Israel?

Who were the Patriarchs?

Where did Abraham first live?

Where did Moses first have a revelation of God?

What was the new name of God revealed to Moses?

Where did the Israelites make a covenant with God?

What was in the Ark?

What language did Jesus speak?

Who was king when Jesus was born?

What does the name Christ mean?

What is the meaning of Gospel?

Why did Jesus go to Jerusalem?

Who gave the order for the Crucifixion?

What happened at Pentecost?

Where was Mohammed born?

What is the Kaaba?

What is fixed in its wall?

Name Mohammed's parents.

Who was Mohammed's wife?

What was the Migration?

How did Mohammed take Mecca?

Where did Zoroaster live?

What name did he use for God?

Where did he finally find success?

How did Zoroaster die?

THE CALL OF MOSES

Moses was keeping the flock of his father-in-law, Jethro, the priest of Midian; and he led his flock to the west side of the wilderness, and came to the mountain of God. And the angel of the Lord appeared to him in a flame of fire out of the midst of a bush; and he looked, and lo, the bush was burning, yet it was not consumed. And Moses said, 'I will turn aside and see this great sight, why the bush is not burnt'. When the Lord saw that he turned aside to see, God called to him out of the bush, 'Moses, Moses!' And he said, 'Here am I.' Then he said, 'Do not come near; put off your shoes from your feet, for the place on which you are standing is holy ground.' And he said, 'I am the God of your father, the God of Abraham, the God of Isaac, and the God of Jacob' . . . And God said to Moses, 'I AM WHO I AM.' And he said, 'Say this to the people of Israel, "I AM has sent me to you." '

Exodus 3:1–6, 14

THE DEATH OF MOSES

Moses went up from the plains of Moab to Mount Nebo, to the top of Pisgah, which is opposite Jericho. And the Lord showed him all the land . . . And the Lord said to him, 'This is the land of which I swore to Abraham, to Isaac, and to Jacob, "I will give it to your descendants." I have let you see it with your eyes, but you shall not go over there.' So Moses the servant of the Lord died there in the land of Moab, according to the word of the Lord, and he buried him in the valley in the land of Moab opposite Beth-peor; but no man knows the place of his burial to this day.

Deuteronomy 34: 1, 4–6

THE BAPTISM OF JESUS

In those days Jesus came from Nazareth of Galilee and was baptised by John in the Jordan. And when he came up out of the water, immediately he saw the heavens opened and the Spirit descending upon him like a dove; and a voice came from heaven, 'Thou art my beloved Son; with thee I am well pleased.'

Mark 1: 9–11

THE CRUCIFIXION

They brought him to the place called Golgotha (which means the place of a skull). And they offered him wine mingled with myrrh; but he did not take it. And they crucified him, and divided his garments among them, casting lots for them, to decide what each should take. And it was nine in the morning when they crucified him. And the inscription of the charge against him read, 'The King of the Jews.' And with him they crucified two robbers, one on his right and one on his left. . . . And at three Jesus uttered a loud cry, and breathed his

last . . . And when the centurion, who stood facing him, saw that he
thus breathed his last, he said, 'Truly this man was a son of God!'

Mark 15: 22–27, 37, 39

MOHAMMED'S VISION

He stood straight, upon the high horizon,
Then he drew near, and let himself down,
Till he was two bow-lengths off or nearer,
And suggested to his servant what he suggested.

He saw him too, at a second descent,
By the plum-tree at the boundary,
Near which is the garden of the abode,
When the plum-tree was strangely enveloped.
The eye turned not aside, nor passed its limits.
Verily, he saw one of the greatest signs of his Lord.

Koran 53: 6–18

THE DEATH OF MOHAMMED

   The apostle began to suffer from the illness by which God took him
to what honour and compassion he intended for him . . . The apostle
used to say, 'God never takes a prophet to himself without giving
him the choice.' When he was at the point of death the last word I
heard the apostle saying was, 'Nay, rather the Exalted Companion of
paradise.' I said to myself, Then by God he is not choosing us. And I
knew that that was what he used to tell us, namely that a prophet does
not die without being given the choice.

From the Life of the Prophet by Ibn Ishaq

THE CHOICE OF ZOROASTER

The Wise Lord himself spoke, he who understands the prayers in
his soul: 'No master has been found, no judge according to righteousness' . . . (The Good Mind replied): 'I know but this one, Zarathustra
Spitama, the only one who has heard our teaching; he will make known
our purpose, O Wise One, and that of righteousness. Sweetness of
speech shall be given to him.'

ZOROASTER'S SUFFERINGS

To what land shall I flee? Where bend my steps?
I am thrust out from family and tribe;
I have no favour from the village to which I would belong,
Nor from the wicked rulers of the country:
How then, O Lord, shall I obtain thy favour?
. . . To whom will help come through the Good Mind?
To me, for I am chosen for the revelation by thee, O Lord.

The Hymns of Zarathustra, 29 and 46

HINDU SAGES

We said earlier that there was no historical founder of the Hindu religion. There have been many wise men, and it is said that the Hindu scriptures were revealed by God to the ancient sages. There are many holy books, but the three most important collections are the Vedas, the Upanishads and the Gita. The meaning of these names will be explained later when we talk about the holy books of the different religions.

In the Upanishads we read of famous sages, their discussions with kings and teachers, and the questions they asked of their pupils. These are not stories about their lives, but the few names and details simply give the framework of their teaching.

In the Gita there is teaching about Krishna, but not much narrative about him. However, there are many later collections of popular tales, and these include a great deal about Krishna. Many of these stories are confusing, and it is not easy to decide whether Krishna was really a historical figure. He appears as a hero and warrior, also as a teacher of truth, and finally as a revelation (*avatar,* 'descent') of God. Popular stories, however, tell of the birth of Krishna when his parents were threatened by an evil spirit, from which the infant delivered them. In his childhood he played all sorts of naughty tricks on his parents and friends nearby. He grew up in a tribe of cowherds and 'the force of his arms made him famous in the three worlds.' He obtained wonderful weapons from the gods so that he could not be defeated. He took part in the great Indian tribal battles, and acted as charioteer to the principal warrior, giving him advice and teaching as well as victory. Finally he died by being shot in the foot unintentionally by a hunter who mistook him for a deer.

In all this there is not much of the religious teacher. But the Gita makes Krishna a revelation of God, and so he instructs the warrior whose chariot he is driving in all manner of profound truths.

Another hero was Rama, a prince who was exiled from his kingdom with his wife. His wife was stolen by a demon and carried off to Ceylon. With the help of many friends Rama eventually gained his wife back, and also his throne where they lived happily ever after. This story too is made into a model of behaviour and Rama is taken as another revelation of God.

These were revelations rather than teachers. But down Hindu history there have been many teachers of religion and great thinkers, whose teachings are held to be more important than the story of their lives. Six schools of thought were set up by outstanding men, but they are followed more for the truth of what they said than for their deeds. Teachers gathered groups of disciples round them and taught them in quiet places, in the forest or on the banks of a river. Teaching by word of mouth was taken to be more important than reading in a book, and sacred texts were uttered by teachers, learnt by heart by pupils, and passed down by memory through many generations. Still today there are Hindu teachers who gather disciples round them in retreat houses where they live together, discuss, listen and meditate.

Statue of Indian god

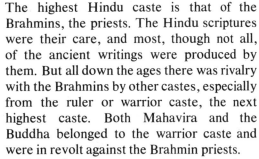

MAHAVIRA

The highest Hindu caste is that of the Brahmins, the priests. The Hindu scriptures were their care, and most, though not all, of the ancient writings were produced by them. But all down the ages there was rivalry with the Brahmins by other castes, especially from the ruler or warrior caste, the next highest caste. Both Mahavira and the Buddha belonged to the warrior caste and were in revolt against the Brahmin priests.

Maha-vira, 'great man', is the title given to the last of the Jinas, the 'conquerors', of the Jain religion in India. It is said that there were twenty-four Jinas, of whom the first lived millions of years ago. The name of the last was Vardhamana, who came to be known as Mahavira, and who lived from 599 to 527 B.C.

Mahavira was born in Vaisali, about thirty miles north of Patna which is on the middle Ganges river. His father was a local ruler and stories are told about his princess mother when the baby was to be born. For fourteen nights she dreamt that she would have a prophet son. When he was born the sky was bright, soft winds swept the earth and all the people were glad. Mahavira was brought up as a nobleman, married and had a baby daughter. His parents were already devoted to the Jain religion, and so severe were some of its ways that after they had confessed their sins they determined not to do anything else that might bring harm or evil, and so they rejected all food and fasted to death.

When he was 30 years old Mahavira decided to leave his home and family and become a wandering holy man like some other Indian teachers. He abandoned everything, even his clothes, and went about begging his food. For twelve years he lived on gifts, never spending more than one night in a village, but passing most of the time squatting in meditation. At last, at the age of 43, light came to him. He was sitting cross-legged, and with arms crossed (as in

many Indian statues), when the truth dawned on him, and he saw 'all conditions of the world, of gods, men and demons—all living things, where they come from and where they go to'. So he became a Jina, a 'conqueror' of life and death.

For the remaining thirty years of his life Mahavira taught his ideas and gathered many disciples round him. He organised a band of men like himself, who were willing to give up all their possessions and all earthly ties to seek the truth. It is said that he had eleven specially close disciples, and that they in turn instructed 4,200 monks.

The monkish order, for men who had abandoned the ordinary way of living, was particularly strong among the Jains. It depended of course upon the gifts of lay people, and it is clear that many thousands of other followers kept to their ordinary way of life and gave alms to support the monks. But in India there always has been a tradition of giving alms to the poor and to holy men. Many rich people gave money and built fine temples.

Mahavira wandered round the middle Ganges region in the dry season, but in the rains he and his monks would live in simple monastery buildings.

In 527 he died or, as they say, he entered Nirvana, 'going out', a state of peace at the top of the universe. Pilgrims still visit the fine temples near Patna where it is said his footsteps may be seen in the stone.

Bronze statue
of Mahavira

BUDDHA

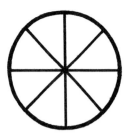

There are some resemblances between the Buddha and Mahavira. They lived about the same time, belonged to the same caste, travelled around the middle Ganges region, and some of the names in their stories are similar.

The Buddha's personal name was Siddhartha, the same as that of Mahavira's father. But he is often called Gautama or Gotama, which was the family name. He lived from about 563 to 483 B.C., a little later than Mahavira, though these dates are not very certain.

Gautama also belonged to the warrior caste, and his father was a ruler of a small kingdom in the foothills of the Himalayas, about 160 km north of Benares. The site of his birth was marked by a pillar put up in the third century B.C., which still survives and has an inscription saying, 'The Blessed One was born here.'

There is a great deal of legend about his birth, more than about any other religious leader. His mother was of surpassing beauty. In a dream she saw a white elephant entering her side and was told that her son would be a world ruler. There were signs in the sky, earthquakes, flowers out of season, heavenly music, and miracles of healing. The child was born as his mother stood under a tree in a park and four gods received the child in a golden net. The babe stood erect, took seven steps, and declared in a voice like a lion, 'I am the chief in the world. This is my last birth. There is now no existence again.'

These stories are fanciful, but there is perhaps more solid matter in the story of Gautama's renunciation. A seer had told the boy's father that he would see four signs: an old man, a sick man, a corpse, and a monk. His father, to prevent this, kept the boy always within the palace grounds and surrounded him with every luxury. The boy was a great athlete and perfect warrior. He married and had a son and

seemed to be content with all that life can give of wealth and happiness.

But when he was 29 years old he went beyond the palace grounds and in due course saw the four signs. This showed him the suffering that there is in the world, sickness, old age and death. The sight of the monk may be meant to show an even greater death to the world, or it may show the peace that can come by living a holy life. In any case, it is clear that the suffering of the world greatly affected Gautama and made him determined to search out its causes and if possible its cure. So he got up in the night, slipped away from his wife and child, and went out on his faithful horse till he reached the limits of his father's domains. Then he abandoned all his belongings, except one robe, and went out as a homeless wanderer.

Gautama went from one Hindu teacher to another trying to find one who would explain the problems of suffering, but without satisfaction. In one village he found five Brahmins who were undergoing a course of extreme fasting. He joined them and fasted so hard that his skin clung to the bones and his ribs stood out like the rafters of a ruined hut, and he fell down as if dead. But when he regained his senses Gautama realised that this was not the way to the truth, and so he took food till his strength was restored. The five Brahmins then left him in disgust.

Gautama continued his search till he came to an old holy town called Gaya, on a tributary of the Ganges. He passed beyond the temples there and finally sat down under a tree which has since been called the Bo-tree, or 'tree of enlightenment' (a pipal tree). He resolved to sit there till truth came to him. It was his darkest time, and he was tempted by an evil spirit, Mara. After a day and a night, light came to Gautama, and he became a Buddha, an 'enlightened one'. He saw the mystery of existence, the cause of suffering, and how to cure it by self-denial. He saw the Four Noble Truths that lead to the destruction of suffering and rebirth, and finally to Nirvana or peace beyond this world.

The tempter tried to persuade the new Buddha to keep this knowledge to himself, while the gods implored him to declare it for the benefit of mankind. Finally he arose and made his way to the great Hindu centre of Benares. On the way he met the five Brahmins who had deserted him. At first they tried to ignore him, but they were struck by his beauty and his teaching and became his first disciples. The Buddha went on, and in a deer park to the north of Benares he preached his first sermon, which is called 'setting in motion the wheel of the doctrine'. This meant the beginning of his teaching, and through it he became a universal ruler, in spiritual things, for his doctrine was intended for all mankind.

The Buddha was now over 35 years of age, and for the next forty or forty-five years he went from place to place in the middle Ganges region teaching and gathering disciples round him. Like Mahavira he only stayed in one place in the rainy season. Although the Buddha's way was called 'the Middle Path', between the extremes of greed on the one hand and fasting on the other, yet his monks did no work but lived on gifts. One day the Buddha appeared at his father's palace, but stood silent with his begging-bowl at the door.

His son became a monk, and his wife also sought to follow him. At first the Buddha was unwilling to admit women to his order, but after appeals from his chief disciple Ananda he allowed women to become nuns with an order of their own. Many stories are told of his wanderings, people he met, Brahmins he conquered in argument, and kings who were converted. But probably the movement remained fairly small, till two centuries later when the emperor Ashoka sent Buddhist missionaries to many countries and put its teachings into his laws.

At last the Buddha felt his end approaching. He is said to have eaten poisoned food, but he was over 80 years old. He gathered his disciples round him and lay down on his side, while he gave them his final instructions. Ananda was weeping and asking what they would do without him. But the Buddha told them to follow his teaching with energy. 'All things are liable to decay, strive with earnestness.' So he passed into Nirvana, and statues show him on his side entering into this peace. His body was cremated, and relics sent to various shrines in the Buddhist world. In 1909 a crystal box was found with small remains said to be those of the Buddha.

Giant stone statues
of dying Buddha and
disciple, Ceylon

**Stone statue of
Buddha, India**

NANAK

Nanak of the Sikhs lived much later than the other Indian teachers we have been learning about, from A.D. 1469 to 1538. His religion arose as a challenge to the Hindu religion with the Moslem faith which had come into India breaking down images, proclaiming faith in one God, but also in some ways akin to Hindu movements of devotion to God.

Before Nanak came Kabir, a poor weaver who lived in Benares. Kabir was a Moslem who was attracted by some things in Hinduism. He hid on the steps that led down to the river Ganges so that a Hindu teacher tripped over him and was forced to accept him as a disciple. Then Kabir went about teaching that there is truth in both the Hindu and the Moslem religions. The leaders of these religions expelled him from Benares, and so he went through the countryside gathering disciples, and composing verses to the love of God. At his death Hindus and Moslems both wanted his body, but it is said that they could only find a wreath of flowers. There are still followers of Kabir today, but others followed Nanak and some of the poems of Kabir are found in the Sikh scriptures.

Nanak was a Hindu who was attracted by Islam. At first he seems to have followed Kabir, but afterwards struck out on his own. One day while bathing in a stream he had a vision, in which God held out to him a cup of sweet nectar. God said to Nanak, 'Go and repeat my name, and make others do so. This cup is a pledge of my regard.' Nanak then composed the Sikh morning prayer which is recited every day (printed on page 40).

Nanak lived in the Punjab, in north-west India, the valley of the river Indus. Here he had his greatest success, though it is said that he travelled far beyond here. One day he went to Mecca, the famous Moslem holy city. Nanak lay down in the courtyard of the Kaaba, with his feet towards the shrine.

When the keeper of the holy place told him this was disrespectful, Nanak replied, 'turn my feet in a direction where God is not to be found.' On another occasion Nanak visited the temple of Krishna at Puri on the coast of the Bay of Bengal (a famous temple called Juggernaut). Here he took part in the evening ceremony of lights before the image, but he gave offence again by declaring that God needed no images.

Nanak, like Kabir, declared that 'there is no Hindu or Moslem.' Like Kabir he composed verses and set them to music. The poet was also a minstrel in those days, and his songs became famous like those of modern popular singers. As other teachers he opposed the authority of the Brahmins; he taught that the caste divisions were wrong in religion, and that men of all castes, and women too, were children of God.

Unlike Mahavira and Buddha, Nanak was opposed to undue fasting and abandonment of the family. He and all the Sikh teachers who followed him were married and taught that true religion was in the heart, and that one could serve God at home as well as in other kinds of work.

Like Kabir, Nanak was claimed by both Hindus and Moslems, but he left the powerful Sikh religion as his true memorial. Sikhs are his 'disciples', and he is their 'teacher' (*guru*).

74

Sikh temple in the Punjab

CHECK YOUR READING

Was there a founder of the Hindu religion?
Who was Krishna?
What do you know about Rama?
How many Hindu schools of thought
  were there?
What does the name Mahavira mean?
How many Jinas were there?
How old was Mahavira when he left home?
Why did he do this?
How many disciples did Mahavira have?
What did they do for a living?
Point out some resemblances between
  Mahavira and Buddha.
What was Buddha's family name?

What were the four signs?
Why did Gautama leave home?
What was the Bo-tree?
What does the name Buddha mean?
Why was the Buddha's way called the
  Middle Way?
Did he admit women to his order?
What did Buddha say as he died?
Who was Kabir?
What did Kabir say about other religions?
Where did Nanak live?
What did Nanak do at Mecca?
What did Nanak say about other religions?
What does the name Sikh mean?

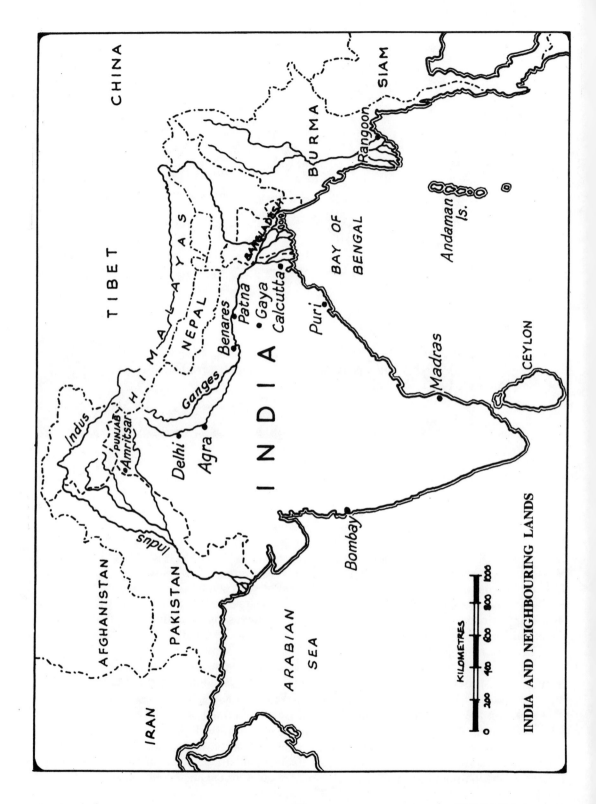

INDIA AND NEIGHBOURING LANDS

SELECTION OF BIOGRAPHIES

THE HINDU SAGE UDDALAKA INSTRUCTS HIS SON SHVETAKETU

Shvetaketu, having become a pupil at the age of twelve, having studied all the Vedas, returned at the age of twenty-four, conceited, thinking himself learned, proud.

Then his father said to him: 'Shvetaketu, my dear, since now you are conceited, think yourself learned, and are proud, did you ask for that teaching whereby what has not been heard of becomes heard of, what has not been thought of becomes thought of, what has not been understood becomes understood?'

'How, pray, sir, is that teaching?'

'Just as, my dear, by one piece of clay everything made of clay may be known, the reality is just "clay" — so, my dear, is that teaching.'

'Do you, sir, tell me it.'

'So be it, my dear,' said he.

From the Chandogya Upanishad

LORD KRISHNA EXPLAINS HIS COMING INTO THE WORLD

Whenever there is a decline of righteousness and rise of unrighteousness, then I send forth myself. For the protection of the good, for the destruction of the wicked, and for the establishment of righteousness, I come into being from age to age.

From the Gita

PRINCE RAMA, EXILED BY HIS FATHER, IS IMPLORED BY HIS MOTHER

'O Righteous One, if thou art established in righteousness, then remain here, serve me and acquire virtue. There is no higher duty than the service of a mother. I am, with the king, equally the object of thy reverence, and I command thee not to go to the forest. In thy separation there is no occasion of rejoicing, neither do I desire to live.'

Seeing his mother, the queen, thus lamenting, the righteous Rama spoke to her dutifully, saying: 'O Holy One, I cannot disregard my father's commands, therefore I bow before thee and entreat thy favour and sanction to enter the forest. Virtue is the highest good on earth. Truth and virtue are one. My father's command is founded on right. I cannot, therefore, disregard my father's command.'

From the story of Rama

MAHAVIRA'S PURITY DURING HIS WANDERINGS

As water does not cling to a copper vessel, or ointment to mother of pearl, so sins found no place in him. His way was free like that of life; like the sky he wanted no support, like the wind he knew no obstacles. His heart was pure like the water of rivers in autumn. Nothing could soil him, like the leaf of a lotus. His senses were well protected like those of a tortoise, he was single and alone like the horn of a rhinoceros. He was free like a bird, brave like an elephant, strong like a bull, difficult to attack like a lion, steady and firm as a mountain, deep like the

77

ocean, mild like the moon, shining like the sun, pure like excellent gold.
Like the earth he patiently bore everything. Like a well-kindled fire he
shone in his splendour.   *From the Kalpa Sutra*

GAUTAMA TELLS HOW HE SOUGHT OUT THE MEANING OF LIFE

Thus, O monks, before my enlightenment, being myself subject to
birth I sought out the nature of birth, being subject to old age I sought
out the nature of old age, of sickness, of death, of sorrow, of impurity.
Then I thought, 'what if I myself, having seen the wretchedness of the
nature of birth, were to seek out the unborn, the supreme peace of
Nirvana'.

While yet a boy, a black-haired lad in the prime of youth, in the first
stage of life, while my unwilling mother and father wept with tear-
stained faces, I cut off my hair and beard, and putting on yellow robes
went forth from a house to a houseless life.

GAUTAMA BECOMES AN ENLIGHTENED BUDDHA

As I thus knew and thus perceived, my mind was freed from sensual
desire, from desire for existence, and from ignorance. In me, now freed,
arose the knowledge of my freedom. I realised that rebirth is destroyed,
the religious life has been led, done is what was to be done, there is
nought for me beyond this world. Ignorance was dispelled, knowledge
arose. Darkness was dispelled, light arose. So is it with him who abides
vigilant, strenuous and resolute.   *From the Tripitaka*

KABIR PRAYS IN POVERTY
I cannot concentrate on my devotions to thee
When I am faint with hunger.
Take back, Lord, this rosary.
I have never been really greedy.
The Divine Name is the only thing I really hanker for.
Kabir says: My inner self is happy,
And when this is so, then I recognise God.

NANAK IS CALLED TO PRAISE GOD
Sing thou, O Nanak, the psalms
Of God as the treasury of sublime virtues.
If a man sings of God and hears of him,
And lets love of God grow within him,
All sorrow shall depart;
In the soul, God will create abiding peace.

If I knew him as he truly is
What words could utter my knowledge?
Enlightened by God, the Teacher has unravelled one mystery:
'There is but one Truth, one Bestower of life;
May I never forget him'.
                    From the Sikh scriptures

CONFUCIUS

The greatest of Chinese wise men was Confucius. His name in Chinese was Kung Fu-tse, 'Master Kung', which Jesuit missionaries made into Confucius. He lived from 551 to 479 B.C., in that Golden Century which stretched right across the world. China had an ancient civilisation, going back to the time of early Mesopotamia and Egypt. By the time of Confucius it was well developed and he came to bring order and better teaching.

Many stories were told later about the origins and infancy of Confucius. It was said that he came from a noble family or even was descended from the ancient kings. When he was born it is said that dragons and 'spirit maidens' flew in the air round about. But Confucius himself said in the only short book that is genuine, 'When I was young, I was without rank and lived in humble circumstances.'

Confucius was born in north central China

Confucius

at a town called Tsou, in the state then called Lu, in what is now south-west Shantung province. His father and mother are not named in the early books, though a later story calls his father Shu He. It is likely that he became an orphan while quite young, like Mohammed. Confucius married and had a son and daughter, but very little is known about these either.

Confucius was poor and did not have much property, but he was educated and had time to practise archery and music. His family had probably come down in the world, but his early struggles gave Confucius a sympathy with common people which was of great value to his teaching. He did not have regular schooling, but he was intelligent and learnt from various teachers, and from the clerical work that he did as a young apprentice.

Confucius was one of the cleverest men of his time, but he had not read many books, for there were not many books written. He wrote some and his followers wrote others. But books in China at that time were written on thin strips of bamboo, fastened together with cords, and so books were heavy and scarce. Printing was first invented in China, but over a thousand years later, and early books were all written by hand. But Confucius had read some of the old histories of China, and he learned by heart some of the traditional poems.

By his reading and thinking Confucius came to believe that he could improve the world in which he lived. China was divided into small states which were often at war with one another, and there were warrior chiefs and brigands who lived by helping

79

one side or another, or helping themselves at the expense of honest people. Governments were badly run; the officials were inefficient and dishonest. Confucius saw that only by seeking the good of the whole people could the government be properly run. He believed that he was called by 'Heaven' to bring about a reform of society. Unlike other teachers we have been learning about, Confucius was not a teacher of religion. He was rather a political and moral teacher. But he firmly believed that his work and his teaching had come from God. 'Heaven begat the good that is in me' was one of his favourite sayings.

Confucius was not successful in getting rulers and governments to listen to him, so he became a teacher. By training young men he saw that he would eventually succeed in producing honest people. His first school was probably more like a debating society, but he was always Master Kung, the obvious leader. In time he came to have many disciples; twenty-two are mentioned in one place, and others elsewhere. These disciples became very fond of him, though he treated them strictly, rebuked them for laziness and laughed at them for stupidity. He told them the way would be hard, but if they were honest and hard-working they could make a new world of justice and peace.

His students got good jobs, and at least ten of them held public office. The rulers of north China were glad to have men on whom they could rely, even though their master had denounced the greed and idleness of aristocrats. In fact the disciples were more successful than their master in getting high positions. Later stories tell of greater success for Confucius, and say that rulers came to consult him. But it seems more likely that his disciples used their influence to secure him some official reward, and that he became a member of the Council of the State of Lu.

Confucius was not satisfied with the small amount of recognition that he had received. He always got on better with young men than with old, and his school had become famous. But when he was 60 years old he got tired of teaching, and he set off on a journey, to try to find some ruler who would give him a job more fitted to his abilities. It is said that he visited a number of towns and had small posts offered to him. But his ideals were too high and he turned them down. After some years he returned home in disappointment.

He spent the rest of his life in teaching and writing. There were a number of history and poetry books that needed setting in order, and it is believed that Confucius had a hand in preparing some of these. In later years they were called the 'Confucian Books' or 'Classics' (see page 126).

Confucius died in 479 B.C. When he was in his last illness one of his disciples asked, 'Shall I pray for you?' Confucius replied, 'I prayed a long time ago.' After his death it is said that his disciples mourned for three years at his grave. Confucius had always stressed the duty men should pay to their fathers, and to their ancestors, and he had paid careful attention to the ancestral ceremonies. So to his disciples Confucius was 'the uncrowned king', the 'teacher of ten thousand generations', and he had the right to the highest reverence.

In later centuries Confucius was greatly honoured, and rulers who had ignored him during his life came to speak his praises. It is said that the Duke of Lu built a temple for the grave of Confucius, and later emperors came and bowed there. Later still it was ordered that sacrifices should be made to Confucius in every school in China.

But the temples of Confucius were under the control of the scholars (mandarins), and had no priests. Scholars were trained to learn the Confucian Classics, and for jobs in the public service boys had to pass examinations in these books.

Confucius is the most famous of all Chinamen, and though his teaching has not always been followed it has been revived again and again. Even today his tomb has been restored (in 1962), and it bears the inscription, 'Confucius, the Primal Sage'.

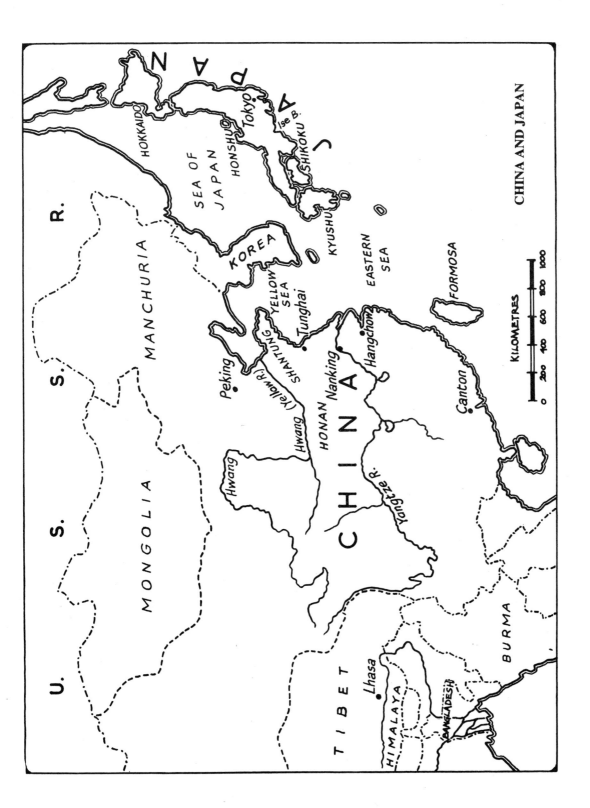

CHINA AND JAPAN

81

LAO TSE

There is a legend which says that Lao Tse was born in 604 B.C. and died 160 years later. But he was already 60 years old when he was born, his hair was white and so he was called Lao Tse, 'Old Master'.

In fact many Chinese and other writers believe few stories that are related about Lao Tse and some think he never existed. His chief importance is the connection, real or supposed, with the great book of the 'Way'. This is the greatest of all Chinese books and is still read and treasured.

If Lao Tse lived it may have been a little before Confucius. Stories say that he was born in a village in Honan province, not far from where Confucius lived. Little is known about his youth, but he spent his later years

in the palace of the emperor, and his son became a great general to whom some later emperors traced their ancestry.

Like Confucius Lao Tse had a school, though he did not advertise it, and people came because they were drawn by its fame. In 517 Lao Tse met Confucius and formed a bad opinion of the younger man, telling him, 'abandon your arrogant ways and countless desires'. This does not seem likely or fair on Confucius, and it is probable that the story was invented by later disciples of the two teachers who quarrelled among themselves. Confucius is said to have gone away from the meeting saying, 'Today I have seen Lao Tse and can only liken him to a dragon.'

After having been keeper of the library or treasury to the court, Lao Tse got disgusted with the corruption of the state and decided to leave it all. Riding in a chariot drawn by a black ox he travelled to the west of China into the mountains. When he got to the great pass on the north-west frontier he was stopped by the keeper of the pass who implored him not to go away without leaving some of his wisdom behind, 'You are about to withdraw yourself from sight. I pray you to compose a book for me.' So it is said that Lao Tse sat down there and then and wrote down the 5,000 Chinese characters that make up the great book of the Way, the Tao Te Ching.

Then he went on his way into the mountains and was never heard of again. He was tempted by evil spirits, but he did not find it hard to resist temptation from ugly or beautiful ones, since they were only 'so many skinbags full of blood'. Finally he ascended into heaven, and pictures in Chinese art show this ascension of Lao Tse.

Lao Tse

82

The story of Lao Tse may have got mixed up with that of another Chinese scholar, Lao Tan, who was a librarian at the royal court some time later. There is another man of similar name who wrote stories about Confucius and wrote a book which has not survived. But the chief importance is the book of the Way. This will be described later.

In Japan there was no founder of the religion, as in India and Africa. Early Japanese stories are full of legends of gods, but not of religious teachers. The greatest teachers appear later, and are Buddhist rather than followers of the national religion of Shinto. Of one of these, Prince Shotoku, who lived in the sixth century A.D., it is said that he was 'greater even than the Buddha who was revealed in India'.

**Lao Tse riding
on an ox**

CHECK YOUR READING

What does the name Confucius mean?

What do you know about the childhood of
  Confucius?

Where was he educated?

What were Chinese books like?

What was the state of China like at this time?

What did Confucius believe about Heaven?

Describe the school and teaching methods of
  Confucius.

How much success did his students have?

What office did Confucius hold?

Why did he leave home?

What were the Classics?

Was Confucius successful in finding a job?

What happened at the death of Confucius?

What kind of honour was paid to the memory
  of Confucius?

What were the examinations for public service like?

What is written on the grave of Confucius?   What do these stories mean?
Relate some of the legends about Lao Tse.   Where did Lao Tse go at the end of his life?
What did Lao Tse say to Confucius?   What book is he supposed to have written?
What did Confucius reply?   What was said about Prince Shotoku?

SELECTION OF BIOGRAPHIES

CONFUCIUS TELLS OF HIS PROGRESS

At fifteen I set my heart upon learning.
At thirty I had planted my feet firm upon the ground.
At forty I no longer suffered from perplexities.
At fifty I knew what were the biddings of Heaven.
At sixty I heard them with docile ear.
At seventy I could follow the dictates of my own heart,
    for what I desired no longer overstepped the boundaries of right.

CONFUCIUS SPEAKS OF ORDER AND MORALITY

Govern the people by regulations, keep order among them by chastisements, and they will flee from you, and lose all self-respect. Govern them by moral force, keep order among them by ritual, and they will keep their self-respect and come to you of their own accord.

He who rules by moral force is like the pole-star, which remains in its place while all the lesser stars do homage to it.

If out of the three hundred Songs I had to take one phrase to cover all my teaching, I would say, 'Let there be no evil in your thoughts.'

From the Analects of Confucius

THE WAY SPEAKS OF THE QUIET STRENGTH OF THE SAGE

Heaven is eternal, the Earth everlasting.
How come they to be so? It is because they do not foster
    their own lives;
That is why they live so long.
Therefore the Sage
Puts himself in the background; but is always to the fore.
Remains outside; but is always there.
Is it not just because he does not strive for any personal end
That all his personal needs are fulfilled?

The Sage relies on actionless activity,
Carries on wordless teaching,
But the myriad creatures are worked upon by him.

From The Way and Its Power

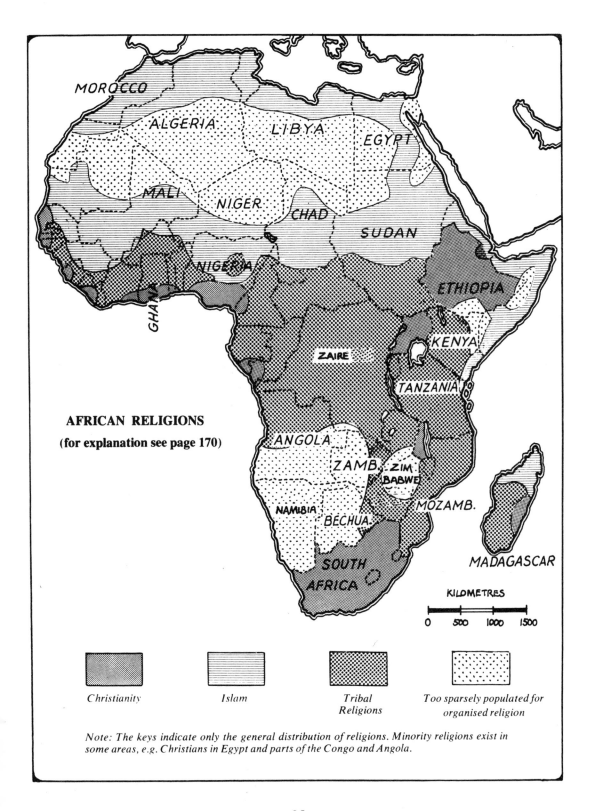

AFRICAN RELIGIONS

(for explanation see page 170)

KILOMETRES

0   500   1000   1500

Christianity   Islam   Tribal   Too sparsely populated for
                                        Religions   organised religion

Note: The keys indicate only the general distribution of religions. Minority religions exist in some areas, e.g. Christians in Egypt and parts of the Congo and Angola.

Part 3

HOLY BOOKS AND THEIR TEACHING

All the great religions have Sacred Writings, or 'Scriptures'. This is the reason why they have survived down a long history, because their teachings were written down and preserved from one generation to another.

We have seen that the Founders of the religions all had special teachings and experiences. They gathered round themselves followers or disciples who accepted their teachings. After the death of the founder the disciples carried on his teachings and in due course these were written down, sometimes at once, sometimes after many years.

As all the great founders of religion lived in Asia, so their books are nearly all written in ancient Asian languages. The one exception is the New Testament, which was written in Greek and so spread rapidly across Europe. The old European religions, of Druids and Norsemen, have left no scriptures since the people were illiterate. The same was true of the ancient religions of America, Australia and Africa; however important their teachers may have been at various times, they left no writings behind them and so all have perished.

The people of ancient Egypt and Mesopotamia, Greece and Rome, had religious writings, which have survived whole or in fragments. But these ancient religions disappeared before the more powerful teachings of Christianity and Islam, and so the older writings are only of interest to students of ancient history. They do not concern us here in studying living religions.

Most of the great founders of religion did not write down their own teachings; they were teachers or prophets, rather than authors or scribes. If Moses wrote down the Law, most of the stories about his life and work were written centuries later by scribes. Jesus is said to have written on the ground on one occasion, and he read the lesson in the synagogue, but his teachings were recorded by his followers. It is said that Mohammed could neither read nor write, but the words he uttered were taken down by secretaries.

Nevertheless the Semitic religions (Judaism, Christianity and Islam) have a long tradition of writing and many holy books. But in India writing was scorned by the Brahmin priests, and they passed on their teachings by word of mouth. Pupils learnt them by heart, and so they were carried on from generation to generation by memory. The memory training was very careful and exact, and the teachings were preserved intact. Only after many centuries were they at last written down, but now there are very many Indian holy books. The Jains and the Buddhists too memorised their teachings, but they wrote them down earlier than the Hindus.

In China Confucius was a literary figure of importance, and in addition to his own writings other books were said to have been written by him. But we have seen that Lao Tse was a legendary figure, and here the writings are more important than the man. In Japanese Shinto the scriptures were not written down till the Chinese Buddhists brought the art of writing.

We shall now proceed to look at these sacred writings in turn.

THE JEWISH BIBLE

The word Bible comes from a Greek word meaning 'books', and it is used both for the Jewish and the Christian scriptures. The Bible was written on skin or parchment made up into a roll or scroll. Later copies were written on a kind of paper called papyrus, made from the pith of a plant cut into strips, glued together, and polished. The sheets that were formed were more like a modern book than the parchment roll.

There are many ancient copies of the Bible, but until recently the oldest copies in Hebrew dated from the ninth century A.D., though there were older translations in Greek. But the discovery of manuscripts in the caves by the Dead Sea, the Dead Sea Scrolls, known from 1947 onwards, has revealed Hebrew manuscripts going back to about the second century B.C.

The Jewish Bible was all written in Hebrew, except for a few chapters of the book of Daniel, which were in Aramaic. Hebrew writing was in square letters, reading from right to left, and without vowels in the oldest versions. Hebrew was the language of the people in the olden days, but gradually it became fixed as a bookish language and was replaced by Aramaic for common speech well before the time of Jesus. The Bible was still read in Hebrew in the synagogues, but there were commentaries written to explain it and translations were made. The most famous translation was the Septuagint, from a word meaning 'seventy', because it is said to have been made by seventy translators working on the Hebrew text and turning it into Greek. This was done about 270 B.C. In the New Testament many of the quotations from the Old Testament are taken from this Septuagint Greek translation.

The Jewish Bible is divided into three parts: the Law, the Prophets and the Writings. Of these the most important for Jews is the Law, called the Torah. This is composed of the first five books of the Bible (called Pentateuch in Greek): Genesis, Exodus, Leviticus, Numbers and Deuteronomy. These were said to have been written by Moses, but many modern scholars think that in the form in which we have them now they were written centuries later by scribes. Perhaps Moses wrote the substance of the Ten Commandments and the Book of the Covenant (Exodus 24; see page 54).

The Book of Genesis begins with two versions of creation (Chapter 1—2, 4a; 2, 4b—24); then after various legendary stories it comes to Noah and his descendants traced through his son Shem (the Semites). Then Abraham and his descendants narrow the interest still more to the sons of Jacob, the twelve tribes of Israel. In Exodus the Israelites are led out of captivity in Egypt by Moses, and taken to make the Covenant on Mount Sinai. The other three books of the Torah are concerned with Laws for the priests and people. Deuteronomy means 'second book of the law', and gives a new version for the Jews at a later period.

The books of the Prophets in the Jewish Bible begin with what Christians call the historical books; these are regarded as the Former Prophets: Joshua, Judges, Samuel and Kings. They tell the story of the Hebrews in Palestine, and the later court records are some of the most detailed early historical narratives ever written.

The Latter Prophets are the 'big three'; Isaiah, Jeremiah and Ezekiel, and the 'twelve', from Hosea to Malachi. These prophetic books are among the most important writings of the Hebrews. Beginning with Amos and Hosea they teach 'ethical monotheism', that is to say, moral life and belief in one God. This is developed by Isaiah, and made more personal in Jeremiah. The second part of the book of Isaiah (often called

Scroll of Jewish Bible

Second Isaiah) gives some of the finest Bible teachings, and tells of the Suffering Servant of God.

The Writings include Psalms, Proverbs, Job, and smaller books down to Daniel and Chronicles. The Psalms were the hymns of the Jewish church and have been used by Jews and Christians down the ages to this day. Job is a great debate over the problem of why the righteous suffer; in the introduction and the dialogues in this book several solutions are given as to why men suffer, but in the end it is a mystery.

Daniel was probably written at a late date, to encourage the soldiers of the Maccabees in the second century B.C. who were fighting against the Syrian Greeks who had defiled the temple of God in Jerusalem. Its strange visions have often puzzled Jews and Christians.

Some Hebrew Bibles, but not all, include the Apocrypha. This word means 'hidden writings', and they were written at a late time, in Greek, and not counted as being as important as the rest of the Bible though their stories are useful examples, such as those of Maccabees, Tobit and Judith. The books of Wisdom and Sirach contain lofty teachings, rather like the books of Proverbs or Job.

The Bible is an anthology, made up of different books by many authors at various dates down the long history of the ancient Hebrew people. Many of the books were written by scribes whose names are unknown, and others may bear the name of a prophet, such as Isaiah or Zechariah, but that does not guarantee that he wrote all of it. In ancient times, in many countries, it was the custom to name a book after a great person. It might contain his teaching, or might simply be written by a scribe who admired him. The list of authoritative books for the Jews was fixed about A.D. 100 by a meeting of teachers at Jabneh in Palestine. They fixed the 'canon' or list of books, and the Apocryphal books were outside this.

The Jews had other holy books, of which by far the most important is the Talmud, 'instruction'. This is a very long collection of interpretations of the Bible, instructions about Jewish festivals, laws of personal and social behaviour, further teachings about God, the Messiah, the future life, and the restoration of Israel after much suffering. There were also laws about agriculture, marriage, civil law, and observations about astronomy, medicine and botany.

During their long history, and many sufferings, the Jews cherished the Bible, and guided their lives by its teaching and by the explanations of the Talmud.

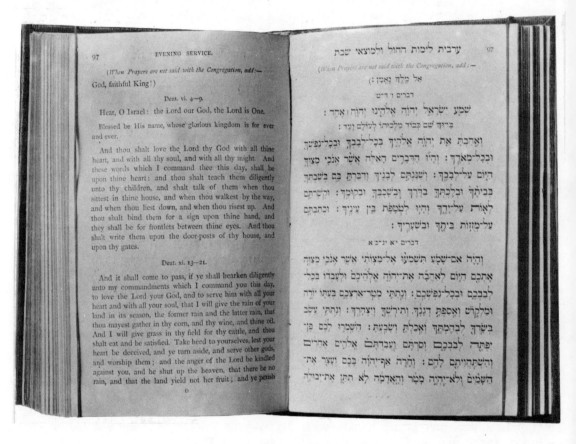

Jewish Prayer Book

FROM THE JEWISH BIBLE
(and see pages 24, 66)

THE TEN COMMANDMENTS

You shall have no other gods before me.

You shall not make yourself a graven image, or any likeness of anything that is in heaven above, or that is in the earth beneath, or that is in the water under the earth; you shall not bow down to them or serve them; for I the LORD your God am a jealous God, visiting the iniquity of the fathers upon the children to the third and the fourth generation of those who hate me, but showing steadfast love to thousands of those who love me and keep my commandments.

You shall not take the name of the LORD your God in vain; for the LORD will not hold him guiltless who takes his name in vain.

Remember the sabbath day, to keep it holy. Six days you shall labour, and do all your work; but the seventh day is a sabbath to the LORD your God; in it you shall not do any work, you, or your son, or your daughter, your manservant, or your maidservant, or your cattle, or the sojourner who is within your gates; for in six days the LORD made heaven and earth, the sea, and all that is in them, and rested the seventh day; therefore the LORD blessed the sabbath day and hallowed it.

Honour your father and your mother, that your days may be long in the land which the LORD your God gives you.

You shall not kill.

You shall not commit adultery.

You shall not steal.

You shall not bear false witness against your neighbour.

You shall not covet your neighbour's house; you shall not covet your neighbour's wife, or his manservant, or his maidservant, or his ox, or his ass, or anything that is your neighbour's.

Exodus 20:3–17

THE LAW OF HOLINESS

You shall be holy; for I the LORD your God am holy.

Leviticus 19:2

WHAT GOD DEMANDS: ETHICAL MONOTHEISM

He has showed you, O man, what is good; and what does the LORD require of you but to do justice, and to love mercy, and to walk humbly with your God.

Micah 6:8

THE NEW COVENANT

Behold, the days are coming, says the LORD, when I will make a new covenant with the house of Israel and the house of Judah; not like the covenant which I made with their fathers when I took them out of the land of Egypt, my covenant which they broke, though I was

91

their husband, says the LORD. But this is the covenant which I will make with the house of Israel after those days, says the LORD: I will put my law within them, and I will write it in their hearts; and I will be their God, and they shall be my people. And no longer shall each man teach his neighbour and each his brother, saying, 'Know the LORD', for they shall all know me, from the least of them to the greatest, says the LORD; for I will forgive their iniquity, and I will remember their sin no more.

Jeremiah 31:31-34

THE COMING KING

There shall come forth a shoot from the stump of Jesse, and a branch shall grow out of his roots.

And the Spirit of the LORD shall rest upon him, the spirit of wisdom and understanding, the spirit of counsel and might, the spirit of knowledge and fear of the LORD.

Isaiah 11:1-2

THE SUFFERING SERVANT OF GOD

He was despised and rejected by man; a man of sorrows, and acquainted with grief; and as one from whom men hide their faces he was despised, and we esteemed him not.

Surely he has borne our griefs and carried our sorrows; yet we esteemed him stricken, smitten by God, and afflicted.

But he was wounded for our transgressions, he was bruised for our iniquities; the chastisement of our peace was upon him, and with his stripes we are healed.

Isaiah 53:3-5

A VISION OF PEACE

They shall beat their swords into plowshares, and their spears into pruning hooks; nation shall not lift up sword against nation, neither shall they learn war any more.

Isaiah 2:4

GOD SHOWS THE LIMITATION OF JOB'S KNOWLEDGE

Then the LORD answered Job out of the whirlwind:
Who is this that darkens counsel by words without knowledge?
Gird up your loins like a man, I will question you, and you shall declare to me.

Where were you when I laid the foundation of the earth?
Tell me, if you have understanding.
Who determined its measurements — surely you know!
Or who stretched the line upon it?

On what were its bases sunk, or who laid its cornerstone, when the morning stars sang together, and all the sons of God shouted for joy?

Job 38:1-7

THE SEARCH FOR WISDOM

Where shall wisdom be found?
And where is the place of understanding?
 . . . Behold, the fear of the Lord, that is wisdom;
And to depart from evil is understanding.

Job 28:12 and 28

THE SOULS OF THE RIGHTEOUS

The souls of the righteous are in the hand of God, and no torment shall touch them.

In the eyes of the foolish they seemed to have died, and their departure was accounted to be to their hurt, and their journeying away from us to be their ruin, but they are in peace.

Wisdom of Solomon 3:1-3

THE WHOLE DUTY OF MAN

Remember also your Creator in the days of your youth, before the evil days come, and the years draw near, when you will say, 'I have no pleasure in them' . . . before the silver cord is snapped, or the golden bowl is broken, or the pitcher is broken at the fountain, or the wheel is broken at the cistern, and the dust returns to the earth as it was, and the spirit returns to God who gave it.

This is the end of the matter; all has been heard.

Fear God, and keep his commandments; for this is the whole duty of man.

For God will bring every deed into judgement, with every secret thing, whether good or evil.

Ecclesiastes 12

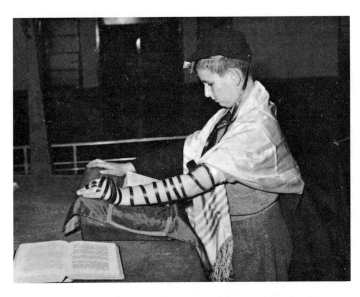

Jewish boy wearing strapped boxes containing portions of scripture

93

Christianity is the only religion that includes the whole scriptures of another religion and reveres them together with its own special writings. Because of this some knowledge of the Old Testament is necessary for all Christians, though they interpret the Old by the New as Jesus himself did.

The Jewish Bible is called by Christians the Old Testament or Covenant, because it tells of the Covenant made with God by the Israelites under Moses at Mount Sinai. The Christian writings are called New Testament or Covenant, because to them is applied the prophecy of Jeremiah (31:31–34) of a New Covenant in men's hearts. This New Covenant was made by Jesus with his disciples in the Last Supper (Luke 22:20).

Most of the first Christians were Jews and all the books of the New Testament were written by Jews, who often quoted passages from the Old Testament in support of their teachings. But they wrote in Greek, which was the common language of trade and government all round the Mediterranean world in the time of Jesus. Jesus spoke in Aramaic, and a few fragments of his Aramaic words remain: talitha cumi, ephphatha (Mark 5:41; 7:34). But his teachings were translated into Greek for the use of Christians outside Palestine as Christianity rapidly spread throughout the Roman Empire.

None of the earliest Christian writings remain, but there are splendid copies made on parchment by careful scribes from the third and fourth centuries and fragments on papyrus from the second century. The two greatest complete copies date from the fourth century; the Vaticanus which is in the Vatican library in Rome, and the Sinaiticus which was discovered at a monastery on Mount Sinai in the nineteenth century and is in the British Museum. All modern translations use these two manuscripts, though they also use other versions and fragments.

The New Testament is divided into four Gospels, the Acts of the Apostles, 21 Epistles or letters, and the book of Revelation or Apocalypse. The 'canon' or list of these books, accepted as authority by the church, was decided in the second century. There were other books written later, 'apocryphal Gospels and Acts', but these are mostly inferior, and contain many legends. There are only a few fragments that compare with the teaching of the New Testament.

The four Gospels give the life and teaching of Jesus according to four different followers. Jesus spoke the Gospel, the Good News, and these four Gospels are selections from his teaching and actions from different angles. It is generally agreed nowadays that Mark was written first, because an early writer says that he wrote down the preaching of Peter, and nearly all of Mark has been

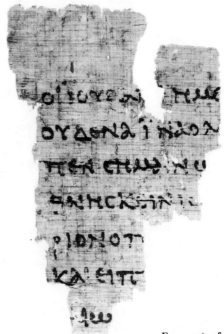

Fragments of

copied into Matthew and Luke. Matthew and Luke also share a collection of Sayings of Jesus, that may have been written in Aramaic by the disciple Matthew. But they add other material, and Luke in particular has favourite stories, such as the Prodigal Son, the Good Samaritan, Zacchaeus, the rich man and Lazarus, and the walk to Emmaus. Matthew arranged his teaching in order, such as the Sermon on the Mount.

The Fourth Gospel, called after John, gives stories about Jesus at the beginning of each chapter, followed by long explanations and other teachings. This is believed to be the last Gospel to be written, about the end of the first century.

The teaching of Jesus in the Gospels was first of all the Good News that the Reign of God was near. Then this was put into practice by healing the sick and calling sinners to repentance. Jesus spoke of God as Father, who forgave men their sins and sent good to all men alike. Those who followed Jesus became the nucleus of a new community, which was open to all races and classes.

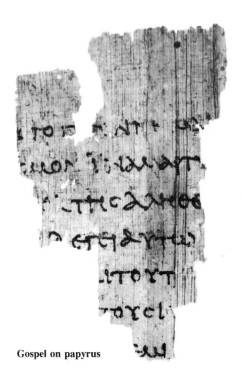

Gospel on papyrus

This soon developed into the Church.

After the Crucifixion of Jesus the disciples were in despair, but this was changed into hope when they had visions of Jesus risen from the dead, and on the day of Pentecost they were inspired to take up his preaching of the Kingdom. This is told in the Book of Acts; first Peter and his companions preached the good news and then, with the conversion of the learned Paul of Tarsus, the Gospel was taken far out into the world outside Palestine. So Paul became the Apostle of the Gentiles.

The Epistles are letters sent by Paul and others to churches like Rome, Corinth and so on, and friends such as Timothy and Philemon. Most of them are more than short personal letters, and they become explanations of Christian belief. They teach faith in Jesus as the Christ, the 'anointed' one of God whom the Jews had been expecting but most of them had not recognised him. Christ was called Son of God, which also meant anointed or chosen, but in addition it came to mean that in Christ believers saw the very nature and love of God. So God the Creator, great and lofty, became known as a God of Love, through the teaching, actions, death and resurrection of Jesus on behalf of all men.

It is not always easy to follow this teaching, partly because Paul dictated most of his letters to secretaries, who could not keep up with his quick pace; and also because Paul had a subtle and involved way of expressing his thoughts. But what emerged was a new way of thinking about God, as revealed in Jesus Christ.

This appears in different form in other Epistles; in Hebrews (which is not by Paul but like his teaching), and in John. John's letters finally bring us to the statement that 'God is love'.

The letter of James is more practical, dealing with problems of Christian living, and in some ways it resembles the Sermon on the Mount.

The book of Revelation was written under the stress of the persecution of Christians

95

by Nero and later Roman emperors. Christians refused to worship images of the emperor and so they were imprisoned and killed. Revelation resembles other books written during times of strife, for example Daniel in the Old Testament. Then it has secret words, such as the 'number of the beast' (13:18) which was probably meant to represent Nero Caesar in Hebrew characters. The strange visions of heaven and warfare must not be taken literally. Many Christians have gone astray down the ages in trying to apply these visions to their own times, and to heaven and hell. But they are a kind of picture writing, and can only be understood in that way.

The New Testament, especially the Gospels, is the rule of life for Christians. Jesus said that men should not just call him Lord, but do the things that he had taught them.

An illuminated manuscript, John 1:1

FROM THE NEW TESTAMENT
(and see pages 25, 66)

THE BEATITUDES

Blessed are the poor in spirit, for theirs is the kingdom of heaven.

Blessed are those who mourn, for they shall be comforted.

Blessed are the meek, for they shall inherit the earth.

Blessed are those who hunger and thirst after righteousness, for they shall be satisfied.

Blessed are the merciful, for they shall obtain mercy.

Blessed are the pure in heart, for they shall see God.

Blessed are the peacemakers, for they shall be called sons of God.

Blessed are those who are persecuted for righteousness' sake, for theirs is the kingdom of heaven.

Blessed are you when men revile you and persecute you and utter all kinds of evil against you falsely on my account. Rejoice and be glad, for your reward is great in heaven, for so men persecuted the prophets who were before you.

Matthew 5:3–11

LOVE YOUR ENEMIES

Love your enemies and pray for those who persecute you, so that you may be sons of your Father who is in heaven; for he makes his sun to rise on the evil and on the good, and sends rain on the just and on the unjust. For if you love those who love you, what reward have you? Do not even the tax collectors do the same? And if you salute only your brothers, what more are you doing than others? Do not even the Gentiles do the same? You, therefore, must be perfect, as your heavenly Father is perfect.

Matthew 5:44–48

THE GOLDEN RULE

Whatever you wish that men would do to you, do so to them; for this is the law and the prophets.

Matthew 7:12

THE KINGDOM OF GOD

The kingdom of heaven is like a grain of mustard seed which a man took and sowed in his field; it is the smallest of all seeds, but when it has grown it is the greatest of shrubs and becomes a tree, so that the birds of the air come and make nests in its branches.

The kingdom of heaven is like leaven which a woman took and hid in three measures of meal, till it was all leavened.

The kingdom of heaven is like treasure hidden in a field, which a man found and covered up; then in his joy he goes and sells all that he has and buys that field.

The kingdom of heaven is like a merchant in search of fine pearls,

97

who, on finding one pearl of great value, went and sold all that he had and bought it.

Matthew 13:31–33, 44–45

COME UNTO ME

Come to me, all who labour and are heavy-laden, and I will give you rest. Take my yoke upon you, and learn from me; for I am gentle and lowly in heart, and you will find rest for your souls. For my yoke is easy, and my burden is light.

Matthew 11:28–30

GOD REVEALED IN CHRIST

It is God who said, 'Let light shine out of darkness', who has shone in our hearts, to give the light of the knowledge of the glory of God in the face of Christ.

2 Corinthians 4:6

GOD'S PROVIDENCE

We know that in everything God works for good with those who love him, who are called according to his purpose . . . For I am sure that neither death, nor life, nor angels, nor principalities, nor things present, nor things to come, nor powers, nor height, nor depth, nor anything

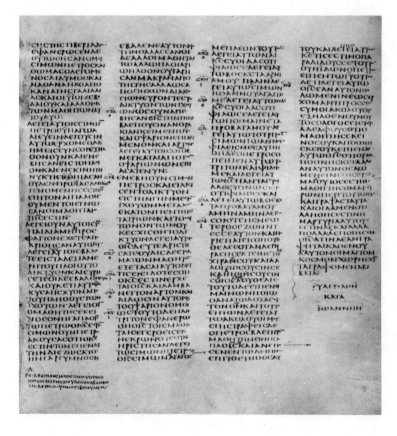

The Codex Sinaiticus

else in all creation, will be able to separate us from the love of God in Christ Jesus our Lord.

Romans 8:28, 38–39

CHRISTIAN LOVE

If I speak in the tongues of men and of angels, but have not love, I am a noisy gong or a clanging cymbal. And if I have prophetic powers, and understand all mysteries and all knowledge, and if I have all faith, so as to remove mountains, but have not love, I am nothing. If I give away all I have, and if I deliver my body to be burned, but have not love, I gain nothing.

Love is patient and kind; love is not jealous or boastful; it is not arrogant or rude. Love does not insist on its own way; it is not irritable or resentful; it does not rejoice at wrong, but rejoices in the right. Love bears all things, believes all things, hopes all things, endures all things. Love never ends . . . Faith, hope, love abide, these three; but the greatest of these is love.

1 Corinthians 13:1–8, 13

CHRISTIAN BEHAVIOUR

Bless those who persecute you; bless and do not curse them. Rejoice with those who rejoice, weep with those who weep. Live in harmony with one another; do not be haughty, but associate with the lowly, never be conceited. Repay no one evil for evil, but take thought for what is noble in the sight of all. If possible, so far as it depends upon you, live peaceably with all. Beloved, never avenge yourselves, but leave it to the wrath of God; for it is written, 'Vengeance is mine, I will repay, says the Lord.' No, 'if your enemy is hungry, feed him; if he is thirsty, give him drink; for by doing so you will heap burning coals upon his head.' Do not be overcome by evil, but overcome evil with good.

Romans 12:14–21

GOD IS LOVE

God is love, and he who abides in love abides in God, and God abides in him . . . If any one says, 'I love God', and hates his brother, he is a liar; for he who does not love his brother whom he has seen, cannot love God whom he has not seen. And this commandment we have from him, that he who loves God should love his brother also.

1 John 4:16, 20–21

FAITH AND ACTIONS

What does it profit, my brothers, if a man says he has faith but has not works? Can his faith save him? If a brother or a sister is ill-clad and in lack of daily food, and one of you says to them, 'Go in peace, be warmed and filled', without giving them the things needed for the body, what does it profit? So faith, by itself, if it has no works, is dead.

James 2:14–17

THE MOSLEM KORAN

The sacred book of the Moslems is the Koran, which means 'recitation'. It is believed that this was sent by God through the angel Gabriel, who revealed it to Mohammed over a period of twenty years. Thus the Koran is regarded as the Word of God, which was eternally in heaven, and was given to Mohammed in the Arabic language.

Mohammed 'recited' the Koran. It is believed that he could not read or write, and so the Koran was no book of his own invention. The writing came later, perhaps partly during Mohammed's life, but mostly after his death. It is said that after Mohammed's death his successor or 'caliph', Abu Bakr, gave orders for a secretary called Zaid to collect the writings and memories of the Koran. This he did 'from pieces of paper, stones, palm-leaves, shoulder-blades, ribs, bits of leather, and from the hearts of men'. This means that some fragments were written down, on different kinds of material, while others were kept in men's memories.

About twenty years later the third caliph, Othman, finding that there were differences in various Korans, gave orders for an official version to be made. Zaid did this and the official version was then sent to the chief Moslem towns, and variant versions were destroyed. This means that all Korans are still the same, though there are a few differences in old commentaries.

The Koran is not an easy book to read, and there are several reasons for this. It is written in Arabic, and in a kind of rhymed prose. This means that in translations the rhyme disappears, and so the chanting which Moslems love is not possible. Then the order in which the chapters of the Koran are arranged makes reading difficult. After the first chapter, the Opening prayer (quoted on page 24), the Koran is arranged with the longest chapters first, reducing gradually till the short ones are reached. So Chapter 2 has 286 verses, while Chapter 110 has only 3. Some English translations (Everyman and Penguin) reverse this order, and put the shorter chapters first, and this makes for easier reading.

All Moslems learn the Koran in Arabic, even if that is not their own language. At least they know the prayers and some short chapters by heart, and many Moslems know the whole book by heart. Translations are permitted today, for private use, but not for use in the mosque.

The Koran is about the same length as the New Testament. It has 114 chapters (*suras*). Some of these are headed Mecca and some Medina, indicating that they were revealed to Mohammed when he lived at Mecca from 610 to 622, or at Medina from 622 to 632. The short chapters were mostly uttered by him at Mecca. They are brief, forcible prophecies, telling of the oneness of God, calling men to serve him, and abandon their idols, and warning of coming judgement. The chapters of Medina are longer, and many of them are concerned with the life of the Moslem community there, its questions of property, marriage, work and war.

Every chapter of the Koran but one begins with the sentence, 'In the name of God, the Compassionate, the Merciful.' God is spoken of many times as judge, king, wise, powerful, but always his compassion and mercy are stressed. The chapters of the Koran are numbered in most translations, but in Arabic they have names, according to some person or thing mentioned in them, like Abraham, Joseph, Mary, the Cow, the Bee, the Unity.

Mohammed gave the Koran to the Arab people as a heavenly book for them. There were Jews and Christians in Arabia in his

Title page of a Koran

time, and these had their holy books, the Law and the Gospel. So Mohammed always had respect for these holy books, and he called Jews and Christians 'the People of the Book'. Moslems should always pay respect to these books, and those who follow their teachings, even if they differ with them over some beliefs.

A number of people from the Bible are named in the Koran, and stories told about them that are similar to Bible stories though with some differences. Adam, Abraham, Joseph, David, Solomon and others are all called Prophets, and they are honoured as true messengers of God.

The Koran mentions Jesus over twenty times, and always speaks of him with reverence. The story of Mary and the birth of Jesus is twice recounted, as in Luke's Gospel though with some differences. Jesus is said to have healed the sick, given sight to the blind and raised the dead. There is a version of the Last Supper. But the Crucifixion seems to be denied, apparently because it was thought that God would not allow the Jews to kill his Christ, but 'God raised him up to himself'. The Koran emphasises the Unity of God, and so opposes some ideas about the Trinity. But these are beliefs in taking 'Jesus and his mother', as 'gods beside God', which is not the Christian doctrine of the Trinity. Christians are said to be 'nearest in love' to Moslems, and the devotion of their monks in the Arabian deserts is admired, though it is felt that the monkish life is not the best.

The Koran teaches that there is only one God, whose name is Allah in Arabic. The worst sin is to 'associate' any creature with the creator, to worship him. This teaching was directed against the many gods and goddesses of pagan Mecca. Man is the servant or creature of God, whose duty is 'submission', which makes him a Moslem, a submitted man. Those who do not submit, or worship other gods and idols, are warned of the coming judgement of God. Some of the early and short chapters of the Koran are full of vivid pictures of the coming end of the world, the darkening of the sun and sky, the raising of the dead, heaven for the righteous and hell for sinners. Later and longer chapters do not change this picture, but they are concerned more with the life of the Moslem community in Medina, and the laws necessary for good behaviour. Moslems are allowed four wives, in exceptional circumstances, but most Moslems today have only one wife.

The Koran is the great holy book of Islam. But there are also other important teachings, and especially the Traditions (Hadith) which contain many stories of Mohammed and his companions, their life and words.

Verses from the Koran

FROM THE KORAN
(and see pages 24, 67)

MOHAMMED'S CALL TO RECITE THE KORAN
Recite in the name of thy Lord who created,
  created man from clotted blood.
Recite, for thy Lord is the most generous,
  who taught by the pen,
    taught man what he did not know.

96:1–5

O thou clothed in a mantle, rise and warn;
Thy Lord magnify, thy garments purify,
  the wrath flee,
    bestow not favour to gain many,
    for thy Lord wait patiently.
When comes the trumpet-blast,
That will then be a difficult day,
For the unbelievers far from easy.

74:1–10

THE REVELATION OF THE KORAN
Lo, we have sent it down in the Night of Power.
Who has let thee know what is the Night of Power?
The Night of Power is better than a thousand months;
In it the angels and spirits let themselves down, by the permission of
  their Lord, with regard to every affair.
It is peace until the rising of the dawn.

95

THE UNITY OF GOD
Say: 'He is God, One,
God, the eternal;
He brought not forth, nor has he been brought forth,
Equal with him there has never been any one'.

112

GOD'S CARE
By the morning brightness,
By the night when it is still,
Thy Lord has not taken leave of thee, nor despised thee.
The last is better for thee than the first;
Assuredly in the end thy Lord will give thee to thy satisfaction.
Did he not find thee an orphan and give thee shelter?
Did he not find thee erring, and guide thee?
Did he not find thee poor, and enrich thee?
So as for the orphan, be not thou overbearing;
And as for the beggar, scold not;
And as for the goodness of thy Lord, discourse of it.

93

RELIGIOUS DUTIES
Serve God, and do not associate anything with him.

Show to parents kindness; also to relatives, orphans, and the poor, to the person under your protection whether he is a relative or not, to the companion by your side, to the follower of the way, and to whoever your right hands possess. Verily God does not love any crafty boaster.

4, 40

MARY AND JESUS
Recall when the angels said: 'O Mary, God gives thee tidings of a word from himself whose name is the Messiah, Jesus, son of Mary, an eminent one in this world and the hereafter, one of those brought near. And he will speak to the people in the cradle and as grown man, one of the upright.'

She said: 'My Lord, how shall I have a child, seeing no man has touched me?' He said: 'So shall it be, God creates what he wills; when he decides upon a thing, he simply says, "Be" and it is.'

Jesus said: 'I have come to you with a sign from your Lord . . . and I shall heal the blind, and the leprous, and bring the dead to life by the permission of God, and I shall announce to you what you may eat, and what you may store up in your houses; verily in that is a sign for you, if you are believers. Verily, God is my Lord and your Lord, so serve him, this is a straight path.'

3: 40–44

THE COMING JUDGEMENT
When the heaven shall be rent,
when the stars shall be scattered,
when the seas shall be made to boil up,
when the graves shall be ransacked,
A soul shall know what it has sent forward, and what kept back.

82:1–5

TRUE RELIGION
It is not virtuous conduct that you should turn your faces towards the East or the West, but virtuous conduct is that of those who have believed in God and the Last Day, and the Angels, and the Book, and the Prophets; and who, though they love their wealth, bestow it upon relatives, and orphans and the poor, upon the follower of the way, and the beggars, and for the ransoming of captives; who observe the Prayer and pay the Alms; those who fulfil their covenant when they have entered into one, who endure steadfastly under adversity and hardship and the time of attack – these are the ones who have spoken truth, they are the ones who show piety.

2:172

THE LIGHT OF GOD

God is the light of the heavens and the earth;
His light is like a niche in which is a lamp,
    the lamp in glass and the glass like a brilliant star,
    an olive neither of the East nor of the West,
    whose oil would almost give light even though no fire touched it;
Light upon light;
God guides to his light whomsoever he wills.
God coins parables for the people, and God knows everything.
God has permitted houses to be raised and his name to be remembered
    there, in which men give glory to him in the mornings and the
    evenings, men whom neither trade nor bargaining divert from the
    remembrance of God, the observance of Prayer and the paying
    of Alms.

24: 35–37

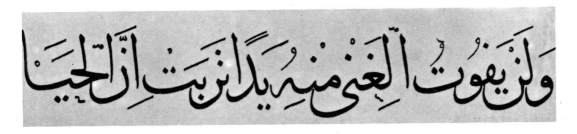

Fragment from the Koran

CHECK YOUR READING

What does the word Bible mean?

On what material were the first scriptures written?

What were the Dead Sea Scrolls, and when were they discovered?

In what language was the Jewish Bible written?

What was the Septuagint?

What are the three parts of the Jewish Bible?

Who were the Latter Prophets?

What is the meaning of Apocrypha?

What is the Talmud?

What does New Testament mean?

In what language was the New Testament written?

What language did Jesus speak?

What is the meaning of the 'canon' of scripture?

Name stories that are found in Luke's Gospel only.

How many Epistles are there?

Where did Paul come from and what was his special task?

Where is the sentence 'God is love' to be found?

What is the book of Revelation about?

What does the word Koran mean?

In what language is it written?

Who wrote down the Koran?

How many chapters are there in the Koran?

What sentence is written at the beginning of each chapter?

Who were the 'People of the Book'?

What does the Koran say about Jesus?

What other holy books do Moslems use?

HINDU VEDAS

The holy books of the Hindus are very long and complicated. The oldest are the Vedas, and others that followed are called Vedanta, 'the end of the Vedas'. The word Veda means 'knowledge' (related to our word 'wit'). So these are books of sacred knowledge.

It was said earlier (page 87) that the Indian priests did not write down their teachings for centuries, but learnt them by heart and so passed them down by memory. This means that there are no very old manuscripts of the Vedas; the oldest were written only a few centuries ago. Various museums have some fragments from about the twelfth century A.D.

Hindus claim, however, that their teachings are very ancient. They are believed to have been revealed to sages in bygone times by the gods themselves. The earliest probably go back to about 1200 B.C., around the time when the Hebrews were beginning to write down the earliest parts of the Old Testament.

The Vedas, and most other Hindu sacred books, are in Sanskrit, the classical language of ancient times which nobody speaks nowadays. Sanskrit is related to Greek and Latin, and there are even resemblances to some English words. The alphabet is different, in squarish letters with a line along the top, but it is written from left to right as in European languages, and not right to left as in Hebrew and Arabic.

The oldest Vedas are in four books, of which the most important is the first, the Rig Veda or 'Veda of praise'. This is a collection of 1,017 hymns to the gods of the Aryan invaders of India, tribes that came down through the passes of the Himalaya mountains about 1500 B.C., shortly before the Exodus of the Israelites from Egypt. These ancient Indians worshipped many gods, and the Vedas are the hymns sung by their priests as they offered sacrifices of oil on fires in the open air or in houses.

These hymns to the gods may seem strange to modern men, but Hindus interpret them as parables of the spiritual life. One god, Varuna, ruler of heavens and seas, has fine hymns addressed to him and he gives laws to men. A Song of Creation, at the end of this

इन्द्रस्येन्द्रियमनस्य रसं सोमस्य भक्षं सुरयासुरो नमुचिरह-
रत् । सो ऽश्विनौ च सरस्वतीं चोपाधावच्छेपानो ऽस्मि न-
मुचये न त्वा दिवा न नक्तं हनानि न दण्डेन न धन्वना न पृ-
थेन न मुष्टिना न शुष्केण नार्द्रेणाथ म इदमहार्षीं दिदं म
आ जिहीर्षेति । ते ऽब्रुवन्स्तु नो ऽत्रायथा हरामेति । सह
न एतद्था हरत्येत्यब्रवीत् । इति तावश्विनौ च सरस्वती च
अपां फेनं वज्रमसिञ्चन्न शुष्को नार्द्रे इति । तेनेन्द्रो नमुचे-
रासुरस्य व्युष्टायां रात्रावनुदित आदित्ये न दिवा न नक्तमि-
ति शिर उद्वासयत् । तस्मादेतद्धिषणाभ्यनूक्तमपां फेनेनेति ।

A Hindu
scripture

106

Reciting
and teaching
texts by
the Ganges

collection, suggests that behind the gods was something even they did not know about.

Other priestly texts came after the Vedas, and then came the Upanishads, the 'end of the Vedas' (Vedanta). Upa-ni-shad means 'down near sitting'. These were discussions or debates of Hindu teachers (*gurus*) who sat down on a river bank or in the forest, with groups of disciples round them who asked questions and listened to instruction. These teachings were gathered into books and passed down the ages. Some of the books are in prose, others in verse, and all in Sanskrit language.

The Upanishads give some of the most important teachings of the Hindu religion. First of all they say that the many gods of the Vedas are really one. There is a spiritual power behind them all, called Brahman. Brahman means 'holy power', and this is the force that keeps the universe going; it is energy, light, life and mind. Brahman brings the world into existence and gives life to man. In fact Brahman is so close to the soul of man that it is almost the same.

There is a famous story in the Upanishads of a boy who was taught by his father the real truth, deeper than what he had learnt at school from the priests. This deep truth is that he is united with the spirit of the universe, the Brahman. As salt cannot be distinguished from water, so the human soul cannot be distinguished from the divine. 'You are yourself that very thing.'

The Upanishads also introduce the teaching of rebirth, the transmigration or passing of the soul from one life to another. When the body dies, the soul goes to the heavenly regions, but after a time it returns to the earth. It is born in a better or worse state according to the life lived before on earth; those whose lives were good rise up in the scale of life. Those who were evil can sink to the animal level. After many rebirths, the soul may escape to 'salvation'.

The Vedas laid great stress on knowledge, as the sure 'way' to salvation. But not all people were learned, so other ways were open to them. There was the 'way of works' (*karma*); by many good actions people could be saved. Others followed a path of severe exercise and discipline. This was Yoga.

Yoga is related to our word 'yoke', and it is the yoking or controlling of body and mind. The Yogi, practitioner of Yoga, sits in an upright position, usually with legs crossed, body perfectly still, gaze fixed, breathing controlled. Then he concentrates his thoughts, stills all care and wandering, and thinks of some teaching, some object or image. Or he may seek to clear his mind altogether of thoughts, and achieve complete blankness and peace. Many men spend hours every day for long periods in this complete self-discipline. Pictures may often be seen of some wild-looking Yogi, a full-time practitioner, who has given up everything for this task.

Ordinary people may practise a little Yoga, but many of them prefer a religion of more warmth and devotion. So there is for them the 'way of devotion'. This is taught in the favourite scripture of Hinduism, the Bhagavad-Gita, the 'Song (Gita) of the Lord'. This is quite a short book, eighteen chapters, about as long as John's Gospel. It teaches devotion to God under the 'incarnation' (*avatar*) of Krishna. This Way of Devotion is open to men and women of all castes, and so is the most popular of all.

These are the most important Hindu sacred books, and all have been translated into English. But there are many others, dating from all periods of Hindu history, some in Sanskrit, others in later popular languages. There are two very long books of epic poetry (*Maha-bharata* and *Rama-yana*), which tell stories of gods and heroes of ancient times. There are long collections of popular tales about the gods. There are books of law and morality, of which the most famous are the *Laws of Manu*, an ancient legendary law-giver. Then there are popular collections of hymns and devotional poetry, which continue the devotion given in the Gita. Through all these Hindu writings run the themes of man's oneness with the divine spirit.

FROM THE HINDU SCRIPTURES
(and see pages 40, 77)

VEDIC HYMN TO VARUNA

He knows the path of birds that fly through heaven, and, sovereign of
the sea, he knows the ships that are thereon.
He knows the pathway of the wind, the spreading, high and mighty
wind;
He knows the gods who dwell above.
Varuna, true to holy law, sits down among his people;
He, most wise, sits there to govern all.
Varuna, hear this call of mine: be gracious to us this day, longing for
help I cry to thee.
Thou, O wise god, art lord of all,
thou art king of earth and heaven;
Hear, and reply with prosperity.

Rig Veda 1:25

FROM THE SONG OF CREATION.

Who verily knows and who can here declare it,
whence it was born and whence comes this creation?

A Yoga posture

109

The gods are later than the world's production.
Who knows, then, whence it first came into being?
He, the first origin of this creation,
　　whether he formed it all or did not form it,
　　whose eye controls this world in highest heaven,
　　he verily knows it, or perhaps he knows not.

Rig Veda 10:129

IN THE BEGINNING

Verily, in the beginning this world was Brahman. It knew only itself: 'I am Brahman.' Therefore it became the All. Whoever of the gods became awakened to this, he indeed became it; likewise in the case of seers, likewise in the case of men. Whoever thus knows, 'I am Brahman' becomes this All.

Brihad-aranyaka Upanishad 1:4

BRAHMAN WITHIN

Verily, this whole world is Brahman. Tranquil, let one worship it as that from which he came forth, as that into which he will be dissolved, as that in which he breathes.

This Soul of mine within the heart is smaller than a grain of rice, or a barley-corn, or a mustard-seed, or a grain of millet, or the kernel of a grain of millet; this Soul of mine within the heart is greater than the earth, greater than the atmosphere, greater than the sky, greater than these worlds.

Containing all works, containing all desires, containing all odours, containing all tastes, encompassing this whole world, the unspeaking, the unconcerned – this is the Soul of mine within the heart, this is Brahman. Into him I shall enter on departing hence.

Chandogya Upanishad 3:14

You do not perceive that the one Reality exists in your own body, but it is truly there. Everything has its being in that subtle essence. That is Reality. That is the Soul. And you are that Soul.

Chandogya Upanishad 6:3

REBIRTH

Those who are of good conduct here – the prospect is that they will come to a pleasant birth, either the birth of a priest, or the birth of a warrior, or the birth of a merchant. But those who are of evil conduct here – the prospect is that they will come to an evil birth, either the birth of a dog, or the birth of a swine, or the birth of an outcaste.

Chandogya Upanishad 5:10

YOGA

Let the yogi constantly try to concentrate his mind, in solitude, self-controlled, free from desires and longing for possessions. He should sit in a clean place, on a firm seat, neither too high nor too low, covered with grass or deerskin or a cloth, one over the other. There taking his place on the seat, concentrating his mind and controlling his thoughts and senses, let him practise yoga for the purification of the soul. Holding the body, head and neck erect and still, looking fixedly forward, without looking round. Serene and fearless, firm in the vow of chastity, subdued in mind, let him sit, harmonised, his mind turned to me and intent on me alone. The yogi of subdued mind, ever keeping himself thus harmonised, attains to peace, the supreme nirvana, which abides in me.

Gita 6:10–15

DEVOTION

Flee unto him for shelter with all thy being. By his grace shalt thou obtain peace and eternal abode. Thus has wisdom more secret than all secrets been declared unto thee by me. Reflect on it fully and do as thou choosest.

Listen again to my supreme word, the most secret of all. Well beloved art thou of me, therefore I shall tell thee what is good for thee. Fix thy mind on me; be devoted to me; sacrifice to me; prostrate thyself before me; so shalt thou come to me. I promise thee truly, for thou art dear to me.

Gita 18:62–65

THE SACRED LAW

Learn that sacred law which is followed by men learned in the Veda and assented to in their hearts by the virtuous, who are ever exempt from hatred and inordinate affection. To act solely from a desire for rewards is not laudable.

Manu 2:1

LIBERALITY

Let him always practise, according to his ability, with a cheerful heart, the duty of liberality, both by sacrifices and by charitable works, if he finds a worthy recipient. If he is asked, let him always give something, be it ever so little, without grudging; for a worthy recipient will be found who saves him. A giver of water obtains satisfaction, a giver of food imperishable happiness.

Manu 4: 227–229

GOD DWELLS IN THE GOOD

Thou dwellest in the hearts of those who have no lust, anger, infatuation, pride, delusion, avarice, excitement, affection or hatred, hypocrisy, vanity, deceitfulness; those who are dear to all, benevolent to all, equable in joy and sorrow, praise and blame, who speak the truthful and the pleasant and are endowed with discrimination, who, while awake or asleep, have taken shelter under thee and indeed have no other resort but thyself.

Tulsidas, Holy Lake of Rama 2: 130

111

JAIN ANGAS

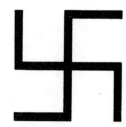

Although the Jains are Indians they do not accept the Hindu Veda scriptures, and have holy books of their own. These are the eleven Angas, 'limbs' or branches.

After the death of their teacher Mahavira the Jains divided into two groups, and these still differ about which are the correct scriptures. As in Hinduism, the teachings were passed on by memory for a long time, and the books of the largest number of Jains were not written down and clearly fixed till about the fifth century A.D. Even so there are not many very old manuscripts that still remain. Many Indian books were written on flat leaves, polished and bound together, and these easily perished.

In addition to the eleven Angas there are other Jain books, differing in each sect. But all Jains are agreed on most of the chief doctrines of their religion.

From a Jain book

112

The basic Jain teaching can be put briefly. It is that the universe is peopled by countless souls. These souls are imprisoned by material bodies and actions. Salvation comes by freeing the soul from matter. After many births the souls may be liberated and go to nirvana, a place of peace at the top of the universe.

The Jains do not give the same importance to God or gods as do the Hindus. For them the gods too, like men, are caught up in the struggle with matter and seek to break free into nirvana. Indeed the best men, the Jinas of whom Mahavira was the latest, are higher than the gods, and the gods have to be reborn as saints before finding release. But the Jains go further, and include the whole of nature in their system. Not only men and gods, but animals, insects, worms, plants and even stones have souls. Thus the whole universe is alive. Because of this the Jains are vegetarians, and refuse to take any animal life at all.

Jains believe that life is ruled by 'deeds' (*karma*), and these deeds decide whether in the next life one goes up higher or descends lower. However, it is only the highest grades of souls which will escape to nirvana, most lower ones can never hope for release. So it is less important to destroy vegetables than to destroy animals. Also, since there are infinite numbers of souls, it will make no difference if some more privileged ones escape from the world altogether into nirvana. The universe will go on revolving, through endless ages, getting worse at times and better again in the cycle of the ages.

Because of their refusal to take life the Jains have been very peaceful, and they make much of their teaching of non-violence. They refuse to go to war, but also they refuse to engage in any occupations which would involve taking life, such as butchery, hunting, or even farming. So they have been mostly traders, and many of them have become rich.

JAIN TEACHINGS
(and see pages 40, 77)

HUMAN BONDAGE

One should know what binds the soul and, knowing, break free from bondage.

What bondage did the Hero declare, and what knowledge did he teach to remove it?

He who grasps at even a little, whether living or lifeless, or consents to another doing so, will never be freed from sorrow.

If a man kills living things, or slays by the hand of another, or consents to another slaying, his sin goes on increasing.

Book of Sermons 1:1

THE ETERNAL LAW

Thus say all the perfect souls and blessed ones, whether past, present or to come – thus they speak, thus they declare, thus they proclaim:

All things breathing, all things existing, all things living, all beings whatever, should not be slain or treated with violence, or insulted, or tortured, or driven away.

This is the pure unchanging eternal law, which the wise ones who know the world have proclaimed, among the earnest and the not-earnest.

Book of Good Conduct 1:4

CHEERFULLY ENDURE

If another insult him, a monk should not lose his temper,
For that is mere childishness – a monk should never be angry.
If he hears words harsh and cruel, vulgar and painful,
He should silently disregard them, and not take them to heart.
Even if beaten he should not be angry, or even think sinfully,
But should know that patience is best, and follow the Law.

Book of Later Instructions 2:24

MORAL VERSES

People speak of high birth and low —
   Mere words, with no real meaning!
Not property or ancient glory makes a man noble,
   But self-denial, wisdom and energy.

This is the duty of a true man —
   To shelter all, as a tree from the fierce sun,
And to labour that many may enjoy what he earns,
   As the fruit of a fertile tree.

Four Hundred Quatrains 195:202

PARSI AVESTA

The most ancient sacred book of the Parsis
is the Avesta, which probably means 'knowledge' like the Hindu Veda. Only part of the
original work remains, preserved in the
liturgy of the temples. The modern Parsis
·do not speak the ancient Persian language,
but still use it in temple services.

It is said that the ancient Avesta was
written in gold ink on ox-hides, and
destroyed by Alexander the Great in his
invasion of Persia in the fourth century B.C.
But it seems likely that the Avestas were
first of all passed on by memory, like the
Hindu Vedas, and only written down much
later. In their present form they date from
about the ninth century A.D.

The oldest parts of the Avesta are the
Gathas or 'songs' (like Hindu Gita). After
this come collections of sacrificial hymns,
and then books of laws and regulations about
purification. · The Gathas are the most
important and we shall only consider these.
They are held to be the work of Zoroaster
himself. He was the great prophet of Persia,
like Moses for the Israelites. But there came
no other prophets after Zoroaster that can
be compared with him, and so his teaching
remained fixed without being developed and
strengthened.

The ancient Persians believed in many
gods, like the Hindu gods. But Zoroaster
rejected all these in favour of Ahura Mazda,
Lord Wisdom, whom he worshipped as the
only true God. Even Mithra, a sun god who
was very popular (and, later adopted by
Roman soldiers, he had temples in Europe)
was banished, though he was allowed back
later as a servant of Ahura Mazda.

**Part of a page
from the manuscript of
the Avesta**

Opposed to Ahura Mazda was an evil
spirit, Ahriman, and it is from him that all
the wickedness of the world comes. The
good God cannot create or permit evil, and
he is constantly at war with the Evil One.
In fact these two great forces, Good and
Evil, are like twins which have always been
struggling for mastery. In the end, however,
the Evil will be bound up, if not destroyed,
and the whole universe will be good and
at peace.

Man has to choose between good and evil.
If he chooses good, then he helps God in his
great struggle against evil. Zoroaster
preached co-operation with God, the establishment of a kingdom of justice on earth.
The alternative was punishment with the
evil spirit.

Zoroaster taught belief in life after death.
The dead would come to a razor-sharp
bridge, and would be weighed in balances.
If the good of their lives outweighed the evil
then they would go to heaven, and cross the
bridge safely. If the evil weighed more
heavily, they would fall to a place of punishment and purification. But after having been
purified these souls also would go to heaven.

The Parsi religion lays great stress on the
good life, because this helps the victory of
Good over Evil. Good thoughts, works and
deeds make the good life and the service
of God.

FROM THE AVESTA
(and see pages 40, 67)

TRUST IN GOD

What help shall my soul expect from anyone,
In whom am I to put my trust as a protector for my cattle,
In whom for myself, in the invocation,
But in the Right, in thee, Wise Lord, and the Best Mind?
I will worship you with praise, O Wise Lord,
Together with Righteousness, Best Mind and the Dominion.

Gathas, Yasna 50

QUESTIONS TO GOD

This I ask thee, O Lord, answer me truly:
Who was the first father of Righteousness at the birth?
Who appointed their path to sun and stars?
Who but thou is it through whom the moon waxes and wanes?
. . . What artificer made light and darkness?
What artificer sleep and waking?
Who made morning, noon and night?
. . . Who made the son reverential in his soul towards his father?
Thus I strive to recognise in thee, O Wise One,
As Holy Spirit, the creator of all things. *Gatha 44*

CHOICE OF GOOD AND EVIL

Now at the beginning the twin spirits have declared their nature, the
    better and the evil,
    in thought and word and deed.
And between the two
    the wise ones choose well, not so the foolish.
Of these two spirits, the evil one chose to do the worst things;
But the Most Holy Spirit, clothed in the most steadfast heavens,
    joined himself unto Righteousness;
    and thus did all those who delight to please the Wise Lord by
    honest deeds. *Gatha 30*

THE BRIDGE OF THE SEPARATOR

Whoever, man or woman, O Wise Lord,
·Shall give me what thou knowest is the best of this existence,
– To wit: reward for Righteousness and the dominion of the Good
    Mind –
And all those whom I shall induce to worship such as you,
With all those will I cross the Bridge of the Separator.
(Those who) destroy existence through evil deeds,
They shall be tortured by their own soul and their own conscience,
When they come to the Bridge of the Separator. *Gatha 46*

GOOD WORKS

He who gives succour to the helpless poor, acknowledges the kingdom
    of God. *Parsi prayer*

116

SIKH GRANTH

The sacred book of the Sikhs, the 'disciples' of Nanak, is the Granth, meaning 'book', (sometimes called Adi Granth, 'first book').

This is a collection of teachings of a number of people, brought together by the fifth teacher of the Sikhs, Arjun, who lived from A.D. 1563 to 1606. It is written in the Punjabi language of north-western India.

There were ten great teachers of the Sikhs, and after the tenth it was said that the Granth would be their teacher (*guru*), and so Sikhs revere it not just as a book but as a living teacher who instructs and inspires them every day. As the Granth is composed of hymns, they are set to music and chanted in the Sikh temples every day.

The Granth is remarkable in that it includes hymns by many Indian teachers, most were Sikhs, but there are also verses by Hindu teachers like Jaidev and Moslems like Kabir. Nanak wrote over 900 hymns, and Arjun who compiled the Granth included over 2,000 of his own verses in the sacred book.

The Sikh religion, as we have seen earlier, comes between Hinduism and Islam, choosing parts of both. It teaches belief in one God, the Name. God is the creator, and he is great, as Islam says. But God is also near to man, and within man, as Hinduism says. Love to God from man is taught, and also God's loving care to men.

The Hindu belief in rebirth is found among the Sikhs, but this is looked upon as a punishment for sin, and God will save men by his grace if they call upon him. Again, in Hindu teaching the world is often thought to be an illusion, not real. But the Sikhs take this to mean that the world hides God from man, if man chooses to do evil things. But good men can see God when they are freed from the impurities of the world.

One of the most important parts of Sikh thought is the need for a teacher (*guru*). Nanak, the founder was the great teacher. After him came nine others, but in each one it was really Nanak himself who was acting, and it is said that each teacher signed his name as Nanak, though they are all known by their personal names as well. After the tenth teacher, the Granth became the Guru, and this is understandable because it contains hymns by all the past teachers. The Indian custom of learning teachings by heart was made easy by those who put their ideas into verses and set them to music. So this religion became popular, in the places where the Punjabi language is spoken.

FROM THE GRANTH
(and see pages 40, 78)

DAILY MEDITATION
As he was in the beginning: the Truth,
So throughout the ages,
He has ever been: the Truth,
So even now he is Truth immanent,
So for ever and ever he shall be
Truth eternal.

Sikh scriptures, p. 28

In the ambrosial hours of fragrant dawn
Think upon and glorify his Name and greatness.
Our own past actions have put this garment on us,
But salvation comes only through his Grace.
O Nanak, this alone we need know,
That God, being Truth, is the one Light of all.

Sikh scriptures, p. 31

THE TEACHER'S HELP

Without the Guru's help we cannot burn
   to nothingness the ashes of self-love;
For the Guru kindles in the human hearts
   the fire of the love of God.

**Sikh scripture showing
Nanak and disciples**

Through the Guru's word alone
  there comes the moment of knowing:
'My Self is that Self'.
Through faith in the Guru the True Self is known.
What else do we need to know?

Sikh scriptures, p. 73

COMPASSION

Let compassion be thy mosque, let faith be thy prayer-mat, let honest
  living be thy Koran, let modesty be the rules of observance, let piety
  be the fasts thou keepest.
In such wise strive to become a Moslem:
  right conduct the Kaaba; truth the prophet, good deeds thy prayer,
  submission to the Lord's will thy rosary;
Nanak, if thou do this, the Lord will be thy protector.

Sikh scriptures, p. 77

RIGHTEOUSNESS

Kabir, where there is divine knowledge there is righteousness:
  where there is falsehood, there is sin.
Where there is covetousness, there is death;
  where there is forgiveness, there the Lord is.

Sikh scriptures, p. 217

CHECK YOUR READING

Name some of the Hindu scriptures.
In what language were they written?
How many Vedas are there?
What do the Upanishads teach?
What is the meaning of rebirth?
Describe the Yoga type of meditation.
What is the Gita?
What does it teach?
Name the Jain holy books.
What do the Jains teach about souls?
Where do they believe souls go when liberated?
What does Karma mean?
Why do Jains refuse to take life?
Name occupations that are forbidden to Jains.

Give the name of the chief Parsi scriptures.
In what language were they written?
What did Zoroaster believe about God?
How did he explain the existence of evil?
What did he think would happen to the evil spirit in the end?
Where did Zoroaster think souls go after death?
Name the sacred books of the Sikhs.
Who collected its chapters together?
Why is it remarkable?
What ideas did the Sikhs take from Islam?
What did the Sikhs say about their teachers?
What teaches them now?

BUDDHIST THREE BASKETS

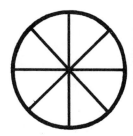

Buddhist teachings, like Hindu, were probably passed on orally at first, but it seems that before very long monks began to write some of them down. However, there are no remains of texts that go back to the first centuries. The first fragments are found in stone monuments put up by the Buddhist emperor Ashoka about 250 B.C. The oldest surviving Buddhist complete manuscript is a copy of the Way of Virtue, written on birch-bark and dating from the second century A.D. After that there are many other writings, from all ages, but these would be copied and altered by scribes who thought they could improve on the originals.

We shall see later that Buddhism soon divided into two great parts. For the moment we shall call these Southern and Northern Buddhism. Southern Buddhism is found in Ceylon, Burma, Siam, Laos and Cambodia. Northern Buddhism is in Tibet, China, Korea, Japan and Vietnam.

The scriptures of the Southern Buddhists are called the Three Baskets (*Tri-pitaka*). These collections of writings are called Baskets in the sense of containers which 'hand on' teachings from one generation to

Monks studying Buddhist texts

120

Tibetan
text

another, as in building baskets are used to pass earth from one builder to another. The Northern Buddhists accept the Three Baskets but they also have further scriptures of their own.

The First Basket is Discipline; this is concerned chiefly with rules for the life of the monks. The Second Basket is the Teaching; this is the most important. The Third Basket is Near-teaching, which means that it contains long explanations and developments of the teaching.

The Teaching Basket contains the doctrines of Gautama the Buddha, and his followers. There are debates with Hindu priests who questioned some of the teachings. There are also stories of the Buddha and other Buddhas before him, descriptions of the Buddha whose body bore thirty-two marks of a superman, and an account of his final descent from heaven to bring his doctrine to the world and become a Buddha, a fully enlightened one.

In discussing the life of the Buddha we saw that at his enlightenment he saw Four Noble Truths. He had been troubled at the suffering of the world, and these truths revealed the cause and cure of suffering. The Four Truths were: (1) all life is suffering, (2) suffering is caused by craving or desire, (3) suffering can be cured by stopping craving, (4) the Eightfold Way, of mental and moral discipline to overcome craving.

The Noble Eightfold Way is basic Buddhist teaching. It is in three groups: (1) Right Views and Right Resolve. This means seeing the truth and resolving to follow it. (2) Right Speech, Right Conduct, Right Livelihood. These show the proper way of living and speaking. (3) Right Effort, Right Mindfulness, Right Concentration or Rapture. These deal with the practice of meditation and adoration.

Also in the Teaching Basket are the Birth Stories and the Way of Virtue. The Birth Stories are 547 tales in which the previous

121

lives of the Buddha are recounted, as bird, animal and man, before his final birth and enlightenment. The Way of Virtue is a little book of moral teaching, which many Buddhists know by heart, and it has been compared to the Sermon on the Mount.

An interesting later writing is the Questions of King Milinda. He is said to have been a Greek ruler who was interested in Buddhism, and asked pointed questions about Buddhist teaching which were efficiently answered by a monk. Buddhism taught about holy men, as did the Jains, rather than gods, but unlike the Jains it denied the existence of a permanent soul. Everything was moving, in the round of rebirth. Karma or 'deeds' linked each birth, bringing a higher or lower state. But there was no soul carried over in rebirth, and in the final state of nirvana nothing remained that could be described in words. Nirvana meant, 'going out', as a flame goes out in the night. So after his final victory the Buddha 'went out', in the sense that he would never be brought back again by Karma. But did he no longer exist? He did exist, but could not be described.

This was very difficult, and in fact nirvana came to be regarded as a state, if not a place, of peace and bliss. There the Buddha dwelt and men adored him.

The Northern Buddhists developed this adoration of the Buddha, and many other Buddhas, much more. They have many additional scriptures. The Diamond Scripture has been preserved in the oldest printed book in the world, dating from China in the ninth century A.D., now in the British Museum. But most important is the Lotus Scripture, or the Lotus of the Wonderful Law. This was written in Sanskrit about the second century A.D., but is very popular in Chinese translation. The Lotus is a symbol of the Buddha and his teaching.

In this book the glorified Buddha appears on a mountain peak in the Himalayas, surrounded by thousands of other Buddhas, gods and disciples. He tells them that the life of the monks is too narrow, only saving a few people. But now he will announce a broad way, or Large Vehicle, of salvation for all mankind. This is a way of faith and grace. Whoever calls upon him by faith, be it man, woman or child, will be saved. The Buddha himself and other heavenly beings are full of compassion to all men.

Northern Buddhism introduces many other heavenly beings, such as Kwanyin, the Lady of Mercy, and Amida the Lord of the Western Paradise. People call on them in daily salutations and prayers.

At the same time, the way of the Buddhist becomes one of compassion to others. The Buddhist does not just seek his own salvation, and many take vows to put off their own nirvana until all beings in the world are saved from their misery and brought to Paradise.

FROM THE BUDDHIST SCRIPTURES
(and see pages 41, 78)

THE FOUR NOBLE TRUTHS
This is the Noble Truth of Suffering. Birth is suffering, age is suffering, disease is suffering, death is suffering . . .
This is the Noble Truth of the Arising of Suffering. It arises from craving, which leads to rebirth, which brings delight and passion, and seeks pleasure now here, now there . . .
This is the Noble Truth of the Stopping of Suffering. It is the complete stopping of that craving, so that no passion remains, leaving it,

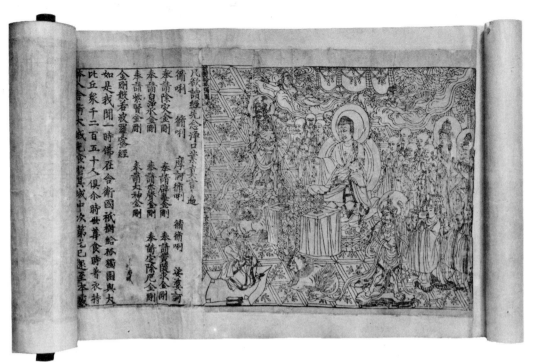

The Diamond Scripture — the oldest printed book in the world

being freed from it, giving no place to it.
This is the Noble Truth of the Way which Leads to the Stopping of
Suffering. It is the Noble Eightfold Path.

THE MIDDLE WAY: THE EIGHTFOLD PATH

The Middle Way of the Teacher avoids both extremes. It is
enlightened, it brings clear vision, it makes for wisdom, and leads to
peace, insight, enlightenment, and nirvana. What is the Middle Way?
It is the Noble Eightfold Path —

Right Views, Right Resolve,
Right Speech, Right Conduct, Right Livelihood,
Right Effort, Right Mindfulness, Right Concentration.

From the Buddha's First Sermon

THE PROCESS OF REBIRTH

King Milinda asked, 'Is it true that nothing transmigrates, and yet
there is rebirth?'
'Yes, your majesty.'
'How can this be? Give me an illustration.'
'Suppose, your majesty, a man lights one lamp from another — does
the one lamp transmigrate to the other?'
'No, your reverence.'
'So there is rebirth without anything transmigrating.'

Questions of King Milinda

123

THE BUDDHA IN NIRVANA

'Does the Buddha still exist?'

'Yes, your Majesty, he does.'

'Then is it possible to point out the Buddha as being here or there?'

'The Lord has passed completely away in nirvana, so that nothing is left which could lead to the formation of another being. And so he cannot be pointed out as being here or there.'

'Give me an illustration.'

'What would your majesty say — if a great fire were blazing, would it be possible to point to a flame which had gone out and say that it was here or there?'

'No, your reverence, the flame is extinguished, it cannot be detected.'

'In just the same way, your majesty, the Lord has passed away in nirvana . . . He can only be pointed out in the body of his doctrine, for it was he who taught it.'

Questions of King Milinda

THE GREAT VEHICLE

Never by a smaller Vehicle
Could a Buddha save any creature.
The Buddha himself is in the Great Vehicle
And accordant with the Truth he has attained
Enriched by meditation and wisdom
By it he saves all creatures.

All Buddhas take the same vow:
'The Buddha-way which I walk,
I will universally cause all the living
To attain this same way with me.'

Lotus Scripture

SUFFERING FOR OTHERS

I work to establish the kingdom of perfect wisdom for all beings. I care not at all for my own deliverance. I must save all beings from the torrent of rebirth with the raft of my omniscient mind. I must pull them back from the great precipice. I must free them from all misfortune, ferry them over the stream of rebirth.

For I have taken upon myself, by my own will, the whole of the pain of all things living. Thus I dare try every abode of pain, in every part of the universe, for I must not defraud the world of the root of good. I resolve to dwell in each state of misfortune through countless ages, for the salvation of all beings.

Compendium of Doctrine

FRIENDLINESS

As a mother cares for her son,
Her only son, all her days,
So towards all things living

A man's mind should be all-embracing.
Friendliness for the whole world,
All-embracing, he should raise on his mind,
Above, below, and across,
Unhindered, free from hate and ill-will.

Second Basket

HATRED AND LOVE
'He insulted me, he struck me,
   He defeated me, he robbed me!'
Those who harbour such thoughts
   Are never appeased in their hatred . . .
But those who do not harbour them
   Are quickly appeased.

Never in this world is hate
   Appeased by hatred;
It is only appeased by love —
   This is an eternal law.

Victory breeds hatred
   For the defeated lie down in sorrow.
Above victory or defeat
   The calm man dwells in peace.

From the Way of Virtue

**Buddhist
monks**

CHINESE CLASSICS

It was said earlier (page 80) that towards the end of his life Confucius is supposed to have edited five Books or Classics. These are the Book of History, the Book of Poetry, the Book of Rites, the Book of Changes, and the Annals of Spring and Autumn. Some people think that Confucius wrote all these, others think that he had nothing to do with them. But either he or his disciples were associated with them, and in time they came to be called the Confucian Classics, the collection of ancient Chinese wisdom. It is possible that Confucius gathered together ancient material in the first four books, and perhaps wrote the fifth one himself.

More important than any of these for knowledge of the life and teaching of Confucius is a little book called the Analects or Selected Sayings (*Lun Yu*). Even this was probably not all written by Confucius, but it is the chief source of historical knowledge about him.

In ancient times the Chinese wrote on thin slips of bamboo, and later on silk, but these were difficult and expensive to use. Tradition says that paper was invented in China by Tsai lun, who died in A.D. 114. He used the bark of trees, thread, old cloth and fishing nets, boiled them together and pounded them to make a paper paste, which was dried and spread out in sheets. Paper became common in China and in the eighth century Chinese prisoners captured by the Arabs brought paper to the Middle East.

Rubbings of stone and seals were early used to reproduce texts. Then wooden blocks were used, especially for Buddhist and Taoist texts. Wood-block printing was widespread in China in the ninth century, and movable type was invented in the eleventh century. This greatly helped the spread of Chinese ideas, but also it became necessary to fix the true texts.

The Confucian Classics had circulated in various versions in the early centuries, and so in A.D. 79 a group of scholars fixed the definitive edition of these works. They were engraved on a series of stone slabs, and at first copied by means of rubbing with ink. But down the ages the correct Confucian texts were preserved on stone tablets in the imperial capital at Peking.

The Analects of Confucius are rather scrappy, consisting of short anecdotes and sayings suitable to the occasion. Confucius taught 'propriety' or the correct moral way of life. He was determined to see that cities were well governed, rulers and elders respected, but also the young and servants protected. He taught kindness to fathers, respect to sons, gentleness to brothers, consideration to husbands and wives, benevolence to rulers, and loyalty to subjects. If all these fulfilled their proper duties, society would live in peace and order.

According to Confucius the best man is the Superior Man, who knows all the duties of life, and performs them as well to those above him as to those beneath. He taught the Golden Mean, or Middle Way between extremes. He was chiefly a teacher of morality, private and public. But he had a religious faith in the guidance of Heaven. He was concerned to pay proper reverence to the spirits of the dead, but he said that we must also do our duty to the living.

'If there is one book in the whole of oriental literature which one should read above all others, it is in my opinion, Lao Tse's *Book of Tao*'. So says the modern Chinese writer Lin Yutang. Whether Lao Tse had anything to do with this book or not (see page 82 above), it is certainly the most original and profoundly religious book ever to come out of China. Still today it is read and treasured by countless Chinese, and kept by many at their bedside at night.

This book is the Tao Te Ching, the Classic of the Way and its Power. The Way (Tao) is a basic Chinese idea, meaning a road or path, and so a way of doing something, a method or principle. There is a Way of heaven, a Way of man, and a Way of rulers, and the Way the universe works. It cannot be defined or fixed, 'The Way that can be told of is not an unvarying Way'. It resembles the Hindu idea of Brahman or God, the holy power, the moving force of the universe. In the Chinese translation of the Bible the 'Word' of John 1:1 is rendered Tao; 'in the beginning was Tao'.

The Book of the Way says that men should live according to nature. So it is opposed to

government interference, and too many laws. Here it came into conflict with the Confucian scholars who were trying to rule people with laws and regulations. No doubt this is the origin of stories about Lao Tse rebuking Confucius.

Being against too much government, it is opposed to warfare, certainly against aggression, and perhaps even defence. Weapons of war should not be collected or cherished, for they are only meant to kill.

The wise man rules through the Way without being known to rule; he teaches without seeming to do so. He works by non-action, or 'actionless activity'. He follows the example of water, which always takes the lowest path, acts quietly, and yet overcomes everything. So the Way never acts, yet all action is done through it.

Part of the manuscript of the Tao Te Ching

127

Down the long history of China, with men suffering from wars, and government oppression, the Way has been a vital element in public and private life. It has softened harshness, and it has been a great inspiration to the masterpieces of Chinese literature and art, as well as the fundamental principle of religion.

FROM CHINESE TEXTS
(and see pages 42, 84)

THE SEARCH FOR GOODNESS

The Master said: 'Without Goodness a man cannot for long endure adversity, cannot for long enjoy prosperity.'

Wealth and rank are what every man desires; but if they can only be retained to the detriment of the Way he professes, he must relinquish them.

Poverty and obscurity are what every man detests; but if they can only be avoided to the detriment of the Way he professes, he must accept them. The gentleman who ever parts company with Goodness does not fulfil that name.

Analects of Confucius 4:2, 5

DUTIES OF RULERS

Duke Ai asked: 'What can I do in order to get the support of the common people?'

The Master said, 'Approach them with dignity, and they will respect you. Show piety towards your parents and kindness towards your children, and they will be loyal to you. Promote those who are worthy, train those who are incompetent; that is the best form of encouragement.'

Analects 2:19—20

CONCERN FOR OTHERS

The Master said: 'Never do to others what you would not like them to do to you.'

Analects 15:23

THE MEAN OR MIDDLE WAY

The Master said: 'Perfect is the Mean in action, and for a long time now very few people have had the capacity for it. I know why the Way is not pursued. It is because the learned run to excess and the ignorant fall short.'

reported by Tzu Ssu

THE INDESCRIBABLE WAY

The Way that can be told of is not an unvarying Way;
The names that can be named are not unvarying names.
It was from the nameless that Heaven and Earth sprang . . .

This same mould we can but call the Mystery,
Or rather the Darker than any Mystery,
The Doorway whence issued all Secret Essences.

Book of the Way 1

The Way is like an empty vessel
That yet may be drawn from
Without ever needing to be filled.
It is bottomless; the very progenitor of all things in the world.
In it all sharpness is blunted,
All tangles untied,
All glare tempered,
All dust smoothed.
It is like a deep pool that never dries.

Way 4

ACTIONLESS ACTIVITY
The Sage relies on actionless activity,
Carries on wordless teaching,

Shrine of Confucius

But the myriad creatures are worked upon by him; he does not
  disown them.
He rears them, but does not lay claim to them,
Controls them, but does not lean upon them,
Achieves his aim, but does not call attention to what he does.

Way 2

AGAINST IMPOSED KNOWLEDGE AND LAWS
Banish wisdom, discard knowledge,
And the people will be benefited a hundredfold.
Banish human kindness, discard morality,
And the people will be dutiful and compassionate.
Banish skill, discard profit,
And thieves and robbers will disappear . . .
Give them Simplicity to look at, the Uncarved Block to hold,
Give them selflessness and fewness of desires.

Way 19

AGAINST WAR
He who by Tao proposes to help a ruler of men
Will oppose all conquest by force of arms;
For such things are wont to rebound.
Where armies are, thorns and brambles grow.
The raising of a great host is followed by a year of dearth.
. . . This is against Tao,
And what is against Tao will soon perish.

Way 30

THREE TREASURES
Here are my three treasures. Guard and keep them!
The first is pity; the second, frugality; the third, refusal to be foremost
  of all things under heaven.'
For only he that pities is truly able to be brave;
Only he that is frugal is truly able to be profuse;
Only he that refuses to be foremost of all things
Is truly able to become chief of all Ministers.

Way 67

TAO THE ORIGIN OF ALL
Tao gave them birth;
The 'power' of Tao reared them,
Shaped them according to their kinds,
Perfected them, giving to each its strength . . .
So you must, 'Rear them, but not lay claim to them.
Control them, but never lean upon them,
Be chief among them, but not manage them.
This is called the mysterious power.'

Way 51

JAPANESE CHRONICLES

When Buddhism arrived in Japan, in the sixth century A.D., it brought with it Chinese culture and the art of writing. In due course these led to the formation and writing down of the Japanese Shinto stories.

The Shinto religion was 'the Way of the Gods' (Shen-Tao). Its earliest stories are long and complicated lists of gods and

The Buddhist Sofugi
temple, Nagasaki

goddesses, but there is little in the way of formal religious teaching about conduct or worship.

The oldest written records date from the eighth century A.D. These are the 'Chronicles of Japan' (Nihongi), and the 'Record of Ancient Things' (Kojiki). These cannot really be called Scriptures, as they were not fixed for religious teaching or worship, and they have little devotional interest. In the tenth century there was compiled the 'Institutes of the Yengi Period', which contain descriptions of some rituals and versions of some prayers.

The Chronicles give long accounts of the gods and goddesses who were at the beginning of things. Finally there emerge two of them who created the Japanese islands. Then Amaterasu, the Sun-goddess, appears. She retires to a cave before the threats of the Storm God, but eventually emerges to restore light to the world. From her descend the Japanese emperors, the first of whom is dated at 660 B.C.

At the end of the Chronicles Buddhism is shown as arriving in Japan. Buddhism eventually took over most of the religious life of the country, and this domination lasted for over a thousand years. This retarded the growth of Shinto from being

131

more than a kind of nature worship. But in the eighteenth century there was a Shinto revival, in reaction against Buddhism and Chinese culture. Motoori and Hirata were two of the chief writers in this revival, and they tried to develop and purify Shinto teaching.

Meanwhile Japanese Buddhism had developed its own special forms, largely working on Chinese ideas. One of the most famous of these, though not the largest, is the Zen Buddhist school (see page 164). Zen means 'meditation' (from Chinese and Indian words). It teaches that 'enlightenment' will come by meditation, without the aid of books. It also influenced daily life,

through the arts: painting, writing, fencing, flower-arrangement, tea-drinking, Zen Buddhism and Shinto together influenced the Japanese warrior class (Samurai), with their Code of Chivalry (Bushido). This taught hardness and blind loyalty to authority, and was a strange perversion of peaceful Buddhism.

In modern times there have arisen new forms of Shinto, influenced both by Buddhism and by Christianity. These are generally founded by inspired teachers, and they lay stress on social work and worship. The older Shinto remains, however, as a love of nature and reverence for the powers behind it.

FROM THE JAPANESE TEXTS
(and see page 42)

THE SUN GODDESS FIXES HER TEMPLE

The Great Goddess, Amaterasu, said: 'The province of Ise, of the divine wind, is the land whither repair the waves from the eternal world, the successive waves. It is a secluded and pleasant land. In this land I wish to dwell.' In compliance, therefore, with the instruction of the Great Goddess, a shrine was erected to her in the province of Ise.

Chronicles of Japan

THE PRIMACY OF AMATERASU

The True Way is one and the same, in every country and throughout heaven and earth. This Way, however, has been correctly transmitted only in our Imperial Land . . . The 'special dispensation of our Imperial Land' means that ours is the native land of the Heaven-Shining Goddess who casts her light over all countries in the four seas. Thus our country is the source and fountainhead of all other countries, and in all matters it excels all the others.

Motoori, Precious Comb-box 6

In all countries, as if by common consent, there are traditions of a divine being who dwells in heaven and who created all things. These traditions have sometimes become distorted, but when we examine them they afford proof of the authenticity of the ancient traditions of the Imperial Land. There are many gods, but this god stands at the centre of them and is holiest of all.

Hirata, Summary of the Ancient Way 1

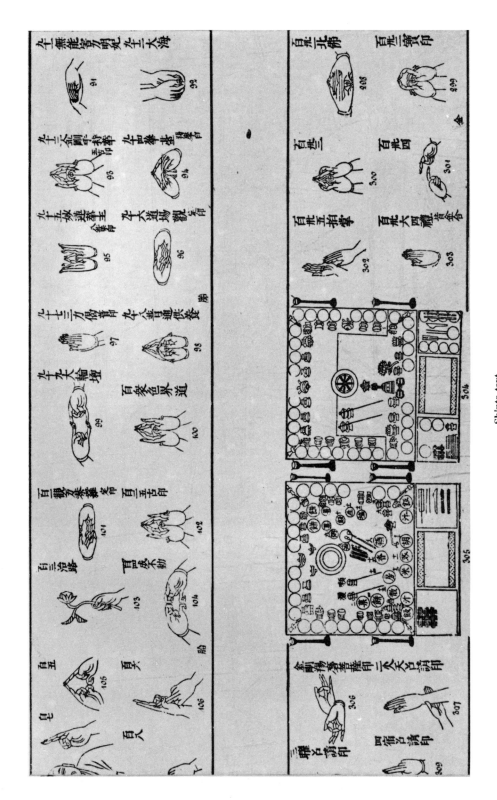

Shinto text
showing ritual actions

133

THE SACRED DANCE

Sweep away all iniquity and save us,
O God of Heavenly Wisdom.
I will speak to you a little while.
Hark and listen to God's word.
I never tell you any evil things.
The creation of heaven and earth was a model of how I created
   husband and wife.
Thus was the beginning of this world . . .
Since the creation I have looked round everywhere in vain to see if
   there was anyone who would understand my Heart . . .
I, your Parent, appear to you all,
   and I explain all things to you in detail.   *Tenrikyo text 1*
                                                         (see page 169)

ZEN SELF-KNOWLEDGE

To study the way of the Buddha is to study your own self. To study
your own self is to forget yourself. To forget yourself is to have the
objective world prevail in you. To have the objective world prevail
in you, is to let go of your 'own' body and mind as well as the body and
mind of 'others.' The enlightenment thus attained may seem to come
to an end, but though it appears to have stopped this momentary
enlightenment should be prolonged and prolonged.

Conversations of Dogen 1

In the pursuit of the Way the prime essential is sitting *(zazen)* . . .
Pass the time in sitting straight, without any thought of acquisition,
without any sense of achieving enlightenment—this is the way of the
Founder.   *Dogen 1*

CHECK YOUR READING

Where are the first fragments of Buddhist teaching recorded?

What is the date of the oldest Buddhist manuscript?

On what material were these texts written?

Name the scriptures of the Southern Buddhists.

In what countries are the Southern Buddhists found?

What were the Four Noble Truths?

What is the Noble Eightfold Path?

What do Buddhists believe about the soul?

Name the most important scripture of the Northern Buddhists.

What is nirvana?

What are the Confucian Classics?

Describe the invention of paper.

Describe the gradual invention of printing.

What is the oldest printed book?

What are the chief sayings of Confucius called?

Name the most important Chinese book.

What is the meaning of the Way (Tao)?

What does the book of the Way teach about government?

What does it teach about warfare?

Give an example of 'actionless activity.'

Name the oldest Japanese Shinto writings.

What are the Chronicles about?

Who were the chief writers of the Shinto revival?

What is the meaning of Zen?

How is it practised?

STATEMENTS OF FAITH

Some religions, but not all, use Statements of Faith or Creeds (beliefs) as useful summaries of their teachings. Christianity especially used these because of many disputes in the early centuries over the correct interpretation of beliefs. The Apostles' Creed was not composed by the first Apostles of Jesus, but appeared in the second century as a summary of what they taught. The Nicene Creed in the fourth century followed on the Council held at Nicea in 325 which tried to define the meaning of the humanity and divinity of Christ. The Athanasian Creed later still was named after Athanasius, one of the foremost orthodox teachers at the Council of Nicea. Most Christians accept the main teaching of these first two creeds, but not all use them in worship.

THE APOSTLES' CREED
  I believe in God the Father Almighty,
  Maker of heaven and earth:
  And in Jesus Christ his only Son our Lord,
  Who was conceived by the Holy Ghost,
  Born of the Virgin Mary,
  Suffered under Pontius Pilate,
  Was crucified, dead, and buried,
  He descended into hell;
  The third day he rose again from the dead,
  He ascended into heaven,
  And sitteth on the right hand of God the
    Father Almighty;
  From thence he shall come to judge the
    quick and the dead.
  I believe in the Holy Ghost,
  The Holy Catholic Church,
  The Communion of Saints,
  The Forgiveness of sins,
  The Resurrection of the body,
  And the Life everlasting.

THE JEWS did not form a creed for many centuries. Their faith was summed up in the Shema: 'Hear, O Israel, the Lord our God, the Lord is One' (see page 16). But in the twelfth century A.D. the Jewish philosopher Moses Maimonides formulated Thirteen Principles of the Faith, and these are printed in the Jewish Prayer Book, for optional use. Here is a summary of them:

I believe with perfect faith that the Creator, blessed be his name, is the Author and Guide of everything that has been created.
I believe that the Creator is a Unity.
I believe that the Creator is not a body, and that he has not any form whatsoever.
I believe that the Creator is the first and the last.
I believe that to the Creator alone it is right to pray.
I believe that all the words of the prophets are true.
I believe that the prophecy of Moses our teacher was true, and that he was the chief of the prophets.
I believe that the whole Law is the same that was given to Moses.
I believe that this Law will not be changed.
I believe that the Creator knows every deed of the children of men and all their thoughts.
I believe that the Creator rewards those that keep his commandments and punishes those that transgress them.
I believe in the coming of the Messiah and, though he tarry, I will wait daily for his coming.
I believe that there will be a resurrection of the dead at the time when it shall please the Creator, blessed be his name, and exalted be the remembrance of him for ever and ever.

THE MOSLEMS also had no detailed creed except the daily Witness: 'I bear witness that there is no God but God. I bear witness that Mohammed is the Apostle of God' (see page 12). This is the first of Five Pillars of faith and practice which are binding on all Moslems. The five are: the Witness, Prayer (five times a day), Almsgiving (to the poor), Fasting (in the month of Ramadan), Pilgrimage to Mecca once at least in a lifetime. But in the tenth century A.D. a great teacher, Al-Ashari, set out two long creeds which were generally held by orthodox Moslems. These are some of the chief points from one of them:

> We acknowledge God, and his Angels, and his Books, and his Apostles, and the revelation they brought from God, and what the trustworthy have related from the Apostle of God.
> We confess that God is one God, and that there is no God at all save him, and that he has not taken to himself any consort.
> We confess that Mohammed is the servant of God and his Apostle, sent by him with Guidance and the religion of Truth.
> We confess that the Garden of Paradise is a reality and the Fire of Hell is a reality.
> We confess that the Hour of Judgement is coming, no doubt whatever about it.

THE PARSIS summarise their faith in a confession which a child makes, together with a priest, at his initiation at seven years of age:

> O Almighty Lord, come to my help. I am a worshipper of Mazda. I praise good thoughts, good words, and good deeds. I believe in the good Mazdayasnian religion, which cuts short discussions and quarrels, which is the dedication of the self, which is holy, and which of all the religions that are, that have yet flourished and are likely to flourish in the future, is the greatest, the best, and the most excellent, and which is the Ahura Mazda Zoroastrian religion.

HINDUS and followers of religions further east do not usually make definite statements of faith. A Hindu is often defined as one who is born into a caste and accepts the authority of the Veda scriptures. Hindu men of upper

Tibetan prayer flag

castes recite daily the verse which is the Mother of the Vedas (see page 26). Others confine themselves to Krishna or another deity.

BUDDHISTS have no creeds but their faith is expressed in the Three Jewels or the Threefold Refuge in the Buddha, the Teaching and the Order (see page 32). Northern Buddhists express their faith in the Nembutsu, 'Adoration to Amida Buddha', and in Tibet in the 'Hail to the Jewel in the Lotus' (see page 34).

136

A Japanese family praying at a shrine

137

Part 4
GROWTH AND PRESENT STATE OF

All religions have a history, though not all have written it down carefully. But in the course of history religions develop, change in some ways, and adapt themselves to different countries and conditions. In outward forms, and some beliefs, Christianity is different in Abyssinia and Scotland, and Buddhism is different in Burma and Tibet. Yet the spirit of their founders may breathe through these differing forms.

The scriptures and statements of faith were compiled centuries ago, but the religions are living forces in the world today. In the first chapter on Men at Prayer we saw something of the worship of the religions, as it is carried on today. In their beliefs and thinking too the religions are living forces, and they are adapting themselves to the ways of thought of modern science.

All religions have grown, though some have extended much farther than others. Some remain almost national or group religions, while others have become world-wide faiths. There are some religions which have disappeared, before the powerful extension of missionary religions like Buddhism, Christianity and Islam. But

RELIGIONS

even when the older religions have disappeared they have often left some marks upon the new faith that has replaced them. Sometimes this has affected their teaching, or it has given rise to new practices in worship or daily life.

After the first founders and their followers, there came other teachers who added to or developed the original teachings. This was part of their living history, for if they had remained unchanged the religions might have died, or they would have been out of touch with changing society. Still today religions look to new teachers to fit their faith to the needs of new societies.

Change might not come for long centuries, and then religions would get set in their ways and often stagnate in their life. But in due course reformers appeared who swept away outworn habits and superstitions. The difficulty in a reformation has been to keep a balance between necessary change and the really essential articles of faith which must be preserved.

In modern times the religions of the world have come into close contact with one another. This is due to the exploration, travel, and ease of communications which make one world of what was formerly divided into East and West, and many smaller fragments. Christianity and Judaism, and to a lesser extent Islam, have been in contact with each other for centuries. But the religions of India and the Far East have only in recent times become known to the West. Buddhism took Indian ideas to the farthest parts of Asia, but only now is Christianity becoming known all over the world.

This new contact of the world's religions with one another brings problems and advantages. We can learn of other ways in which men have sought the truth about human life and the universe. The problems are to learn just what other people mean by the words of their faith. More and more careful and fair study is needed of what other religions teach. Now we are going to take a quick look at their history and present state. We shall see that all religions have different branches and sects, though all try to unite them.

STRUGGLES OF JUDAISM

After the time of Moses and the Exodus of the Israelites from Egypt, the people settled into Canaan, the Promised Land. Judges and kings helped in this settlement which was about completed by the time of David, in 970 B.C. Solomon his son lived in luxury, but he was oppressive and after his death the kingdom broke in two, the northern part being called Israel and the southern Judah.

Palestine was a small country, though it developed a great religion, and the empires at either end of the Fertile Crescent, Egypt and Mesopotamia, invaded Palestine in turn, so that its peoples rarely knew peace. First the kingdom of Israel (Samaria) was destroyed, and then Judah was taken away into exile in Babylon from 586 to 538 B.C. Yet in this time of warfare lived the great prophets, like Isaiah, Jeremiah, Amos and Hosea, who developed the religion of Moses into belief in one God for the whole earth, a God who demanded justice and right from his people.

After the Exile the temple which Solomon had built in Jerusalem, and which had been destroyed, was rebuilt. But the Jews were not yet independent, and they passed under the rule first of the Persians and then of the Greeks. In 166 B.C. they revolted against the Syrian Greek ruler Antiochus who had defiled the temple. Led by Judas the Maccabee, 'the Hammerer', the Jews gained independence and purified the temple, restoring its services which had been interrupted for three years. But in 63 B.C. they came under the rule of the Romans; Pompey took Jerusalem and massacred thousands of Jews.

In the time of Jesus Palestine was divided into several parts, some under Roman governors like Pontius Pilate in Judea, others under some of the Herods, who held their place by favour of Rome. The Jews followed various parties. The Sadducees were the priests at Jerusalem who were subservient to Rome. The Pharisees led the country synagogues and the mass of the people, and were chiefly concerned with religious affairs. The Essenes ('pious ones') were a small sect from whose monastery by the Dead Sea came the famous Scrolls (see page 88). The Zealots wanted to fight the Romans and free their country of them.

In A.D. 66 the Zealots rose in revolt, despite the moderating counsels of Pharisees and Sadducees. Soon the whole land was aflame. The Romans set to work to crush it completely but slowly, and it took four years. In A.D. 70 Jerusalem fell, the temple was burnt, its candlesticks and scrolls carried away and thousands of Jews taken as slaves to Rome. From 132 to 135 another revolt broke out in Palestine, led by Bar Cochba, 'son of the star'. This time the Romans were even harsher. There were huge losses of Jews, and they were forbidden on pain of death to return to Jerusalem. On the site of the devastated Temple a Roman temple was erected to Jupiter.

The Jews were now scattered in 'the Dispersion' and had no national home till the twentieth century. Every day, ever since, Jews have prayed for the restoration of Jerusalem and its temple.

The Sadducees now disappeared, and the Pharisees were left to guard the Jewish religion. About A.D. 100 a group of rabbis, 'teachers', fixed the list ('canon') of true scriptures, and gave regulations for prayers and the calendar of festivals. Soon the Talmud grew up (see page 90), with its many teachings for religious, moral and social life.

The Jews became an ingrown community, guarding their particular laws and customs.

A Jewish rabbi

Their religion persisted because the long line of prophets and teachers had developed its teachings, and suited them to differing conditions. But being ingrown made them appear a strange minority and they suffered persecution, first of all from the Romans, and later from Christians who could not forget that they had been persecuted by Jews at first and Jesus had been crucified by their leaders, though it was the Sadducee priests who had been responsible for betraying Jesus to the Roman governor, jealous of their own position and privileges. The Jewish people and the Pharisees generally had been tolerant of all kinds of prophets and many of them had listened to Jesus with great attention.

During the Middle Ages there arose movements of Jewish 'mystics', teachers of secret or inward revelation, called Cabbalists, 'receivers'. These encouraged Jews in their trials in the Inquisition and other attacks. Freedom came after the Reformation, in countries like Holland and England, where Cromwell allowed the Jews to come and live in peace. The Renaissance and Enlightenment in Europe gradually gave the Jews civic rights and they could become English, French or German. Some became Christians, while others sought to reform Judaism.

The movement of modern or 'liberal' thought that affected Christianity also had

141

its effect upon Judaism. Reform synagogues were built that were different from the Orthodox synagogues. In the Reform there was less Hebrew language used, women could sit with men instead of being kept apart in a gallery, and modern music was used. The Prophets were studied, as well as the Law, and even the Gospels were appreciated by liberal Jews who were ready to see in Jesus the greatest moral teacher of Israel.

Most Jewish synagogues are still Orthodox, though they have adjusted themselves in some ways to modern needs. But both Orthodox and Reform are concerned with the needs of Jews and do not seek to spread their religion outside. They regard missionary work as the task of Christianity or Islam.

Towards the end of the nineteenth century there arose the movement of Zionism, which sought to establish a national home for Jews in Palestine, and the rebuilding of Jerusalem (Zion). Small at first, this increased after the First World War, and especially when Hitler's persecution of Jews sent hundreds of thousands in flight to Palestine. The Arabs lived in Palestine, and Britain ruled under a Mandate of the League of Nations. When Britain withdrew in 1947 fierce fighting broke out between Jews and Arabs. The Jews carved themselves out the kingdom of Israel, west of the Jordan, but not including the old city of Jerusalem which remains Arab. There is a new city, with a Hebrew university. Modern Israel is ruled by Jewish laws, civil and religious. But it only has two million of the twelve million Jews in the world, most of whom live in America, Russia and Europe. Yet in these different countries their faith is the same, in 'the Lord our God, the Lord is One'.

Tunisian Jews studying the Law

142

CHURCH AND CHURCHES

The first Church was largely Jewish, but it rapidly spread into the non-Jewish or 'Gentile' world across the Near East, and into Europe and North Africa. This was largely due to Paul and his followers, who saw that Christianity must be universal.

Like Judaism the Church soon ran into persecution from the Romans. This was because Christians refused to recognise the Roman gods or sacrifice to images of the emperor. Nero blamed his burning of Rome on Christians and from then on Christians were liable to crucifixion, burning, torture, and mauling by wild animals. Paul and Peter were both martyred at Rome, and many other Church leaders suffered in the first centuries. Not all emperors were so harsh, and there were intervals of peace, but Christians were always liable to be de-nounced and imprisoned or killed. Yet despite this Christianity spread far and wide, till in the fourth century it was the most powerful force in the Roman empire. In 312 Constantine, who later became a Christian, gave Christians full liberty of worship. In 380 Christianity became the official religion of the Roman empire.

Outward peace gave the Church time to consider internal differences. There were keen debates about the nature of Christ, his humanity and divinity. In 325 Constantine called the Council of Nicea to provide the true doctrine. But this and later councils, though they gave majority decisions, led to minorities breaking away. In the sixth century the Monophysites held that there was 'one nature' in Christ only, and that divine. They formed the Syrian, Armenian and Coptic (Egyptian and Ethiopian) Churches which still remain.

Next there came struggles for power among the churches. The Eastern Churches claimed to be oldest, and at the Council of Nicea nearly all bishops were from the East. But the bishop of Rome was recognised in time as 'first among equals' because Rome was the centre of the empire. When the empire fell to the barbarians, from 410 onwards, the centre of power moved to Constantinople (Byzantium). Divisions between Rome and Constantinople increased with the centuries, over questions of power and doctrine. Finally in 1053 East and West separated. The Eastern Orthodox Churches remain a federation under different heads or 'patriarchs', with the Ecumenical Patriarch of Constantinople as first. When Russia was converted to Christianity the Russian Church became and remains the largest of the Orthodox Churches.

An Orthodox priest

143

Martin Luther

In the West the power of the Pope ('father') of Rome increased, and there were many struggles with emperors and kings. The Papacy grew powerful, but also corrupt. There were many movements of reform, notably by preaching brothers ('friars') like Francis of Assisi and Dominic. But in the sixteenth century both religious and political unrest led to the Reformation, which began as a movement for purifying the Church, and led to a complete breach. Martin Luther of Germany and John Calvin of France led the Lutheran and Reformed movements which developed into Churches called by those names. The Reformed were opposed to bishops, and preferred Churches to be ruled by Presbyters, 'elders', as in some of the early Churches. In Scotland also nearly all the Churches finally became Presbyterian.

In England the Reformation was more conservative among Anglicans and more reformed among Independents. After the Civil War and Restoration in 1662 the Anglican Church, with its bishops and Prayer Book, was accepted and 2,000 independent ministers were expelled. They became the first Nonconformists, because they did not 'conform' to the state Church and bishops. There were some Presbyterians, as in Scotland. Others came to be called Congregationalists, because they held that each individual congregation or Church should rule itself, and not be subject to a larger organisation or bishop. Yet others were Baptists who believed that only adults, and not children, should be baptized by being fully immersed in water as in the early Church. The Friends (also called Quakers, because they quaked or trembled with the Spirit) had no paid leaders or ministers, no sacraments, and called their Churches 'meeting-houses'; they opposed war and slavery, and worked for social reform.

In the eighteenth century the Methodists taught a life of 'method' in prayer and service, visiting sick and prisoners and starting the great modern missionary movements. Methodism began within the Church of England, but when bishops refused to ordain their ministers the Methodists ordained them in Presbyterian fashion. Thus began another Nonconformist movement. Today they prefer to call themselves Free Churches, and in England Methodism is the largest.

In the nineteenth century a break away from Methodism came with the Salvation Army, which used army organisation, uniform, bands and banners to attract people who were outside the other Churches. The Army works particularly among the poor, and has many social centres. There are many smaller Christian movements. Some of them take the Bible quite literally, like Plymouth Brethren and Four Square Gospel. But Jehovah's Witnesses deny orthodox teachings about Christ and stress more the Jehovah of the Old Testament. In America arose Mormons who use new scriptures introduced by Joseph Smith, and Christian

Scientists who use the writings of Mrs. Eddy and deny the reality of pain and death.

The great variety of Christian Churches is not surprising, for other religions have their divisions, as we shall see. But in this century Christians have come to feel that their divisions are a scandal, and a hindrance to the spread of Christianity. Unions of Churches have been achieved in South India, Canada, Scotland and other places. Conversations towards union have been planned or begun between Roman Catholics and Orthodox, and between Anglicans and Methodists.

The Roman Catholic Church is much the largest of all Churches, with a strong centralized organization. Protestants come next and then Orthodox (see inside back cover). A great feature of modern times is the missionary movement in all the Churches. Christianity began in Palestine, but it spread rapidly over the Near East and Europe. Then it stopped for centuries. But today it is found in all continents and is the largest of all religions. Europe, America and Australasia are nominally Christian. But there are many millions of Christians in Asia and Africa. Christianity seeks to show the whole world the love of God as revealed in Jesus Christ.

**A Salvation Army
open-air meeting**

145

CHART OF CHURCHES

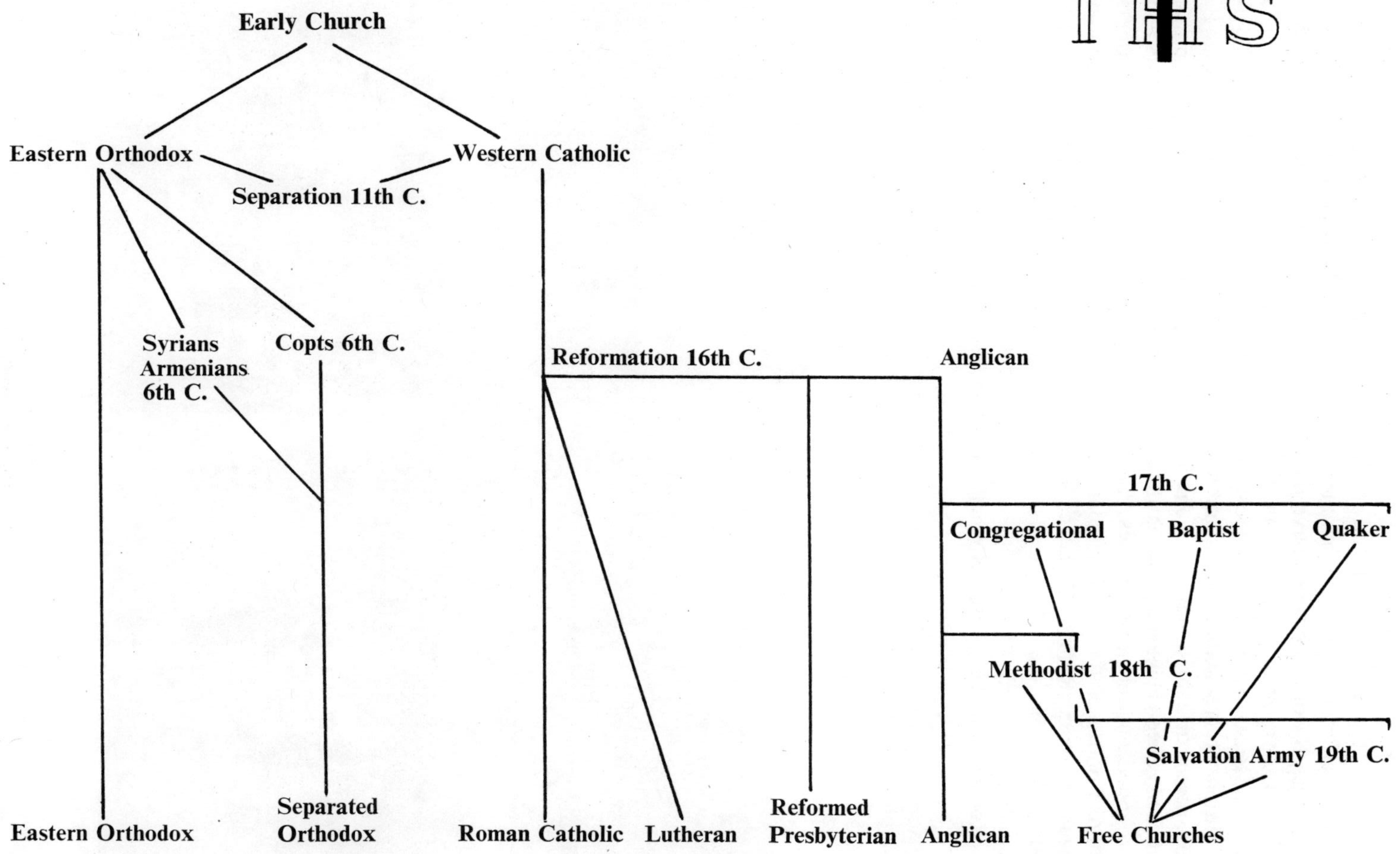

IHS

Early Church

Western Catholic

Eastern Orthodox

Separation 11th C.

Syrians
Armenians
6th C.

Copts 6th C.

Reformation 16th C.

Anglican

17th C.

Quaker

Baptist

Congregational

Methodist 18th C.

Salvation Army 19th C.

Roman Catholic

Lutheran

Reformed
Presbyterian

Anglican

Free Churches

Separated
Orthodox

Eastern Orthodox

SPREAD OF ISLAM

After the death of Mohammed in A.D. 632, a succession of Caliphs, 'successors' or 'deputies', was appointed. The first was Abu Bakr, an old man but one of the first converts. He had to take strong action at once. Bedouin tribes who had sworn loyalty to Mohammed began to break away, and troops were sent to bring them back. Abu Bakr died in 634 but he had reunited Arabia and his armies looked farther afield. He was succeeded by Omar.

Then began the most amazing religious success story of history. No other religion has spread so far in so short a time. The old empires were crumbling. Byzantium (Constantinople) ruled the eastern Mediterranean, and Persia the regions round Mesopotamia. The Arab armies struck at both. South Babylon fell in the year 633, Damascus in 635 and Jerusalem in 637. It is said that Omar visited Jerusalem after his troops had

entered. He saw the site of the old Jewish and pagan temples in ruins, and ordered a mosque to be built there. This is the Mosque of Omar, or Dome of the Rock; this building has often been rebuilt, but it was founded about 690 and is the oldest Moslem building outside Arabia.

The Arab armies entered Egypt in 640 and spread along North Africa. Most of these lands were nominally Christian. Moslems did not normally ill-treat them, and were glad to use them as civil servants, but

Dome of the Rock Mosque, Jerusalem

147

in time these countries became Moslem, with the minority Coptic Church remaining in Egypt. In 711 the Arabs entered Spain, and in 732 they met the armies of the Franks under Charles Martel, at Poitiers in the heart of France. Here the Arabs met their greatest setback. They were thrown back to Spain, though they remained there till the fifteenth century.

In the East the Arabs entered Persia and pressed on to India by 705. In 713 an Arab embassy visited the court of China. Thus in a hundred years from the death of Mohammed the Moslem religion was known from France to China, and it held effective sway from Spain to India. It was, of course, thanks to its armies that Islam spread so rapidly. Idolaters were converted by force, but Christians and Jews were tolerated.

The Arabs were men of the desert, and they conquered lands of high civilisation. In time they absorbed this culture, and when Europe was in the Dark Ages after the fall of the Roman Empire and coming of the Goths, it was the Arabs who preserved Greek medicine, astronomy and philosophy. They learnt paper-making from China and numerals from India, and passed them on to Europe. Arab art, architecture, literature and science were splendid. This was their Golden Age, till the fall of their capital at Baghdad to the Mongol Turks in 1258. But the Turks in due course became Moslems and their empire lasted till the twentieth century.

Meanwhile there had been divisions among Moslems. Omar was succeeded as Caliph by Othman, and he by Ali. All these met a violent death. Ali was cousin and son-in-law of the Prophet but he was opposed by some Moslems and his empire divided.

The followers of Ali broke away and became the Shia, 'followers'. Today Shia Islam is the state religion of Persia and has large followings in Iraq, Syria, Yemen, Pakistan and other lands. The Shia hold the usual Moslem doctrines, but pay special reverence to Ali, and to his son Husain whom they regard as a martyr and celebrate his festival at the beginning of every year.

It is said that there are seventy-two Moslem sects. The Shia are the largest division within Islam, and they have sub-divided into a number of fragments. Most of them are Twelvers, because they follow the first twelve 'leaders' (imams) from Ali and his sons. They hold that the twelfth leader disappeared and will come again at the end of the age as Mahdi or 'guided one'. Other Shia are Seveners or Ismailis, because they hold to only seven leaders, ending at the seventh who was called Ismail, who will return as Mahdi. Some of the Ismailis are called Khoja, from a later leader, and their present ruler is the well-known millionaire the Aga Khan. Yet further divisions include the Druzes, started by Darazi in the tenth century, and now found in Syria.

In modern times the Mahdi expectation gave rise to the Bahais. Their founder the Bab ('door' to the truth) was martyred in Persia in 1850. His successor Baha-ullah established the Bahais, who teach a new universal religion for the modern world, taking ideas from science, and using new forms of prayer.

In the nineteenth century also the Ahmadis arose in India, their founder Ghulam Ahmad being regarded as both Mahdi and Messiah. They are a missionary movement, with centres of education and propaganda in Europe and America, but they are not regarded as orthodox by most Moslems.

The great majority of Moslems, over 80 per cent, call themselves Sunni, followers of the 'path' or tradition. They reject Shia and other teachings. There have not been so many divisions among the Sunni, but in the nineteenth century the revolt of a Mahdi in the Sudan, where General Gordon was killed, was a short-lived attempt at a new Moslem kingdom. In the eighteenth century a man called Wahhab started a Sunni reform in Arabia, and today the Wahhabi sect rules all Arabia and the holy places of Mecca and Medina. It tries to reform Islam by for-

CHART OF MOSLEM SECTS

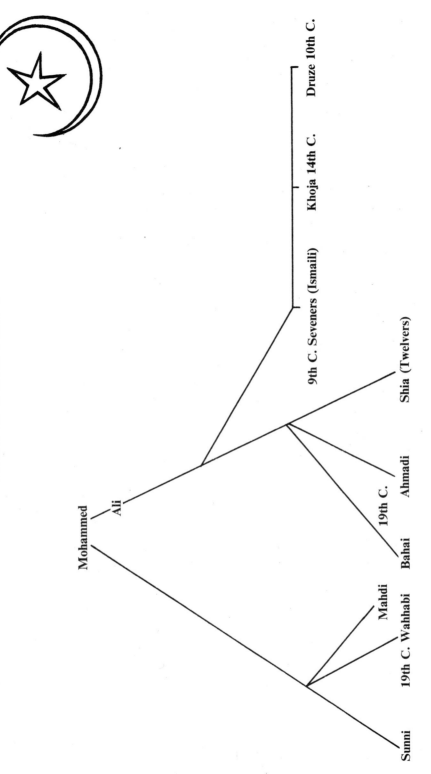

bidding reverence of tombs of saints and the use of alcohol and tobacco. But it also forbids ornaments, music, and games of chance, even chess. It tries to safeguard the purity of ancient Islam by keeping it away from the West. But the rich oil wells of Arabian lands make this very difficult.

Most other Moslem countries try in some degree to come to terms with modern science and ways of living. Turkey, after losing its empire in 1918, abolished the last Caliph in 1924 and became a secular state on the European model. Here and in other lands there have been moves to emancipate women, abolish the veil, forbid or restrict bigamy, and provide Western forms of education. The Koran is translated into modern languages, though Arabic is used in all mosques and set prayers.

Modern Islam is seeking to adapt itself to the modern world, as it did in the past to Greek and Roman culture. But it still remains faithful to its belief that 'there is no god but God, and Mohammed is the Apostle of God'.

**Moslems outside the mosque at
Zaria, Nigeria, on a Friday**

The Taj Mahal, famous Moslem tomb at Agra, India

CHECK YOUR READING

Where and when was the Exile of the Jews?

Who were the Maccabees?

Who were the Essenes?

When did the Jews revolt against the Romans?

What was the Dispersion?

Who were the Cabbalists?

When did the Jews find freedom?

What do Reform Jews teach and practise?

What is Zionism?

Why were the early Christians persecuted?

Who gave them liberty of worship?

What was the purpose of the Council of Nicea?

Why did the Churches of East and West separate?

Who are the Presbyterians?

What do Baptists practise?

When did Methodism start and why?

What does the Salvation Army do?

Where have unions of Churches taken place?

Who were the Caliphs?

Where is the Mosque of Omar and why is it so called?

Describe the spread of Islam in its first century.

What happened in the battle of Poitiers?

Who are the Shia?

What is a Mahdi?

Who are the Bahais?

What do the Wahhabis believe and practise?

151

HINDU VARIANTS

The history of Indian religion is not easy to piece together. In the early period nothing was written down, and at a later date there is such complexity that, as one writer says, it is 'a jungle rather than a building'.

The Veda scriptures belonged to the invading tribes from central Asia, who called themselves Aryans ('noble') and came down into the plains of north-west India about 1500 B.C. (see page 48). But there were already people in northern India, in the valley of the river Indus, who had a high civilisation, comparable to the culture of ancient Mesopotamia and Egypt. From the ruins of their cities that remain we know that these Indus people made images of a Mother Goddess and another god who sat cross-legged like a yogi surrounded by animals. They used the symbol of the swastika, 4,000 years ago. They had large tanks for ritual bathing such as most Hindu temples have today.

These Indus people had a form of writing, which has been preserved on seals that they made, but unfortunately nobody has yet been able to decipher the writing. When the Aryan warriors came down through the passes of the Himalayas, with their horses and chariots, they destroyed the cities of the more peaceable Indus people, and broke up their irrigation system. The outward forms of civilization were overthrown, and for a thousand years there are no traces of such fine walled cities as the Indus people had built. But over the centuries the Aryans mixed with the Indus folk, and their religions became mingled.

The Vedas, composed by Aryan priests or Brahmins, tell of the gods of the sky. Later

Seals from
Indus city

their teachers spoke about Brahman, the 'holy power' in the universe and in man. But these teachers also adopted ideas of rebirth and yoga, which seem to have been held by the Indus people. Also many new gods come in, which were either unknown to the Vedas or join up with one of their gods. Thus Shiva appears, a god who to this day is pictured as a cross-legged yogi, surrounded by animals. His wife is the Mother Goddess (Kali or

Durga or Shakti), whose chief temples are at Calcutta (Kali-ghat, Kali's steps). These are two of the greatest deities of modern India, and to many of their followers they are the only God.

Vishnu was a minor god in the Vedas, but later he became linked with heroes such as Rama and Krishna who were called his

Hindu teachers

'incarnations' or 'descents' (*avatars*). They may have been Indus gods, since Krishna means 'black', and the Indus people were dark-skinned. With these, made into one, Vishnu became and remains the greatest and sole God to millions of Hindus.

Yet underneath all these varieties of deities, the Hindus believe that there is one divine spirit, Brahman. He is the one underlying reality, and gods and images are just ways of picturing him, for the benefit of believers who find it hard to think of him without some kind of image.

But a further problem is the relationship of man to the divine Brahman (see page 107). Many Hindus follow a great teacher, Shankara, who taught that Brahman is everything, and everything is Brahman. This teaching is usually called Pantheism, or Monism, all is God and God is all.

Others, led by a teacher Ramanuja, found that this idea would make it impossible to worship God, for how can one worship oneself? So they teach a Modified Pantheism, believing that God and man are the same nature, but God remains God, and man remains his worshipper.

Yet others are Dualists, holding that God and man are dual, two, and can never be so fully united that there is no difference between them, either of nature or relationship. It is the Modified Pantheists, and the Dualists, who are most concerned with the worship of the different gods and images, though even the Pantheists allow this, as a help to meditation.

Down the ages there were other differences of opinion that affected Hinduism. We have seen that the Buddhists and Jains broke away about the sixth century B.C., to follow their glorified teachers rather than Hindu gods. But Hinduism kept its hold on the Hindu masses, and even revived in powerful movements of devotion. The Jains are still small in numbers, and the Buddhists are far stronger outside India than within it.

From the tenth century A.D. India was invaded and then ruled by Moslems, the Moguls. They were strongly opposed to idolatry, and broke down thousands of Hindu, Jain and Buddhist images and destroyed temples and monasteries. Many Indians became Moslems, but the masses remained Hindu.

European trade and rule came from the sixteenth century. The East India Company wrested power from the Moguls from the eighteenth century, and full British government ruled India from 1857 to 1947.

Under the Moguls Hinduism had become weak and corrupt. Europeans were shocked to see not only idolatry, but blood sacrifices and many excesses. Widows were placed alive on their husband's funeral pyre. Secret Thugs killed travellers in sacrifice to Kali. At the temple of Juggernaut (Jagannatha, a title of Krishna) devotees threw themselves to death under the wheels of the great temple cart. There was need of a great reformation.

Reform could not come from government alone, but Hindu reform societies started which helped to check the gravest abuses. The Brahmo Samaj (One God Society) was founded in 1828, to teach belief in one God, without idols, and adopt readings from other religions in public services. Other societies fought the rigid distinctions of caste in society. The Ramakrishna society was founded in honour of a priest in Calcutta who taught the unity of religions; and schools, orphanages, and temples were built. The poet Tagore founded a university at Shantiniketan. The philosopher Shri Aurobindo founded at Pondicherry an ashram or retreat house which combines meditation with social, educational and craft works. But the most famous reformer was Mahatma ('great-soul') Gandhi (1869–1948). Gandhi worked for Indian independence, but he also tried to reform Hindu religion and liberate the outcastes, whom he called 'God's people'. His methods of Nonviolence have shown the value of Hindu teachings in the modern world.

Mahatma Gandhi spinning cloth

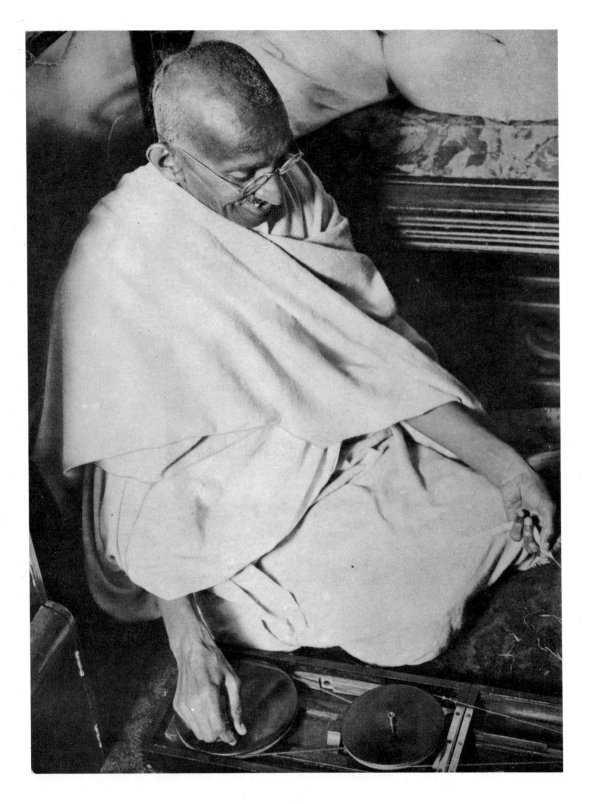

OTHER INDIAN RELIGIONS

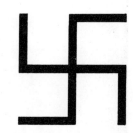

Down their long history the JAINS have divided into two main sects. These are named according to the dress of their monks: 'White-clad' and 'Sky-clad'. The White-clad dress in white robes and live mostly in the colder northern part of India. The Sky-clad live in the hotter south, and at times wear no

clothes because, they say, their teacher Mahavira gave away all his belongings, even to his clothing.

The monks are supported by laymen, and though the Jains have never been very numerous, yet they have succeeded in attracting rich followers who have built splendid temples and even cities on hilltops composed of nothing else but temples. There is a further Jain sect, however, which has no temples or images and worships 'everywhere'.

Jains are strict vegetarians, and monks wear a cloth over their mouths and brush the road before them as they walk, so as to avoid harming any insect. They have 'animal hospitals' attached to their temples, where usually pigeons and other birds are protected and fed. Their teaching of non-violence has inspired other teachers, especially Mahatma Gandhi in modern times.

Though a small minority among the religions of India the Jains have retained their special teachings. They needed reform in modern times, for they had adopted some Hindu gods and customs that were not consistent with their teachings. But education, and a better understanding of their scriptures, have helped in the process of reform.

Jain temple, Calcutta

The history of the PARSI religion after the death of Zoroaster is not clear. The Persian emperors Cyrus and Darius in the sixth–fifth centuries B.C. worshipped the great God Ahura Mazda, but perhaps independently of Zoroaster's teaching. Yet the ideas of Zoroaster spread gradually, as is shown by the many references to him in Greek and Roman literature.

The Persian priests adopted the faith of Zoroaster, though with some changes and some of the old gods appeared again. The priests were the Magi, the 'wise men' of the Bible, who studied the stars as well as engaging in religious and magical practices. In the Christian era Zoroastrianism was the state religion of the Second Persian Empire, from the third to the seventh centuries A.D.

In the seventh century the Moslem Arabs invaded Persia, in the course of their triumphant march across the world. The Persian Empire was overthrown, and this was a serious blow to the state religion. However, the Moslems respected people who worshipped one God and had a holy Book. They extended to Persians the tolerance that they showed to Jews and Christians. But social and official pressure became so great that about a hundred years after the Moslem invasion a large number of Persians decided to emigrate. They moved down the eastern coast, and finally came to India. The tolerant Hindus allowed them to settle and called them Parsis (Persians), a name that they have kept to this day. A few thousand Zoroastrians remain in Persia, called Gabars, 'infidels', by the later Moslems, but now they are adopting the name Parsi for themselves.

In India the Parsis number only just over a hundred thousand people. But they are influential, because of their high level of education, emancipation of women, and the wealth of a small but self-supporting community.

Parsi priests recite the Avesta in the ancient Persian language. Until recently they did not understand it, since it is no longer spoken. But there have been movements of

157

reform. The scriptures are studied in translation, and there are schools for teaching the young. Parsis are tolerant of other religions and seek to follow the Good Life shown to them by Zoroaster.

Cylinder seal showing
King Darius hunting
below Ahura Mazda in a
winged disk

The story of the SIKHS after Nanak is one of struggle and persecution. The fifth teacher Arjun, who compiled the Granth scriptures, also completed the Golden Temple at Amritsar. These two acts infuriated the fanatical Moslem Mogul ruler of India and Arjun was tortured to death. The tenth teacher (*guru*) Govind Singh rebelled against the constant persecution of his religion, and founded the militant Sikh brotherhood (see page 31).

Govind Singh (1675–1708) made an inner circle of initiates, all to be called Singh, 'lion'. They wear beards and turbans, combs, short trousers, daggers and steel bracelets. This was to defend their religion and establish an independent Sikh state. In time the Sikhs dominated the whole of the Punjab.

The Sikhs fought the British fiercely, were defeated in 1849, and then became loyal allies and helped their rulers to put down the Indian Mutiny in 1857. Sikhs became popular among the British for their bravery as soldiers and skill as mechanics. In the Second World War, while other Indian leaders refused to co-operate with Britain, the Punjab government remained loyal. But the Partition of India and Pakistan in 1947 cut right across the Punjab. Sikhs rose in arms to form their own state, and were equally violently attacked by Moslems and Hindus. Finally they were expelled from Moslem Pakistan, after thousands had been massacred. They moved across into India, and fortunately Amritsar was on the Indian side. From time to time the Sikhs have tried by demonstrations and fasting to persuade India to give them more independence, but so far with little success.

With their cities ravaged and many homes ruined the Sikhs set to work after 1947 to repair the damage with characteristic energy. Temples have been repaired and re-gilded and, as in other small communities, Sikhs care for their poorer members. There have been religious reforms too. Various sects had sprung up that disputed the authority of teachers or adopted some Hindu practice

that others rejected. Some writers suggest that Sikhs may merge into Hinduism, but it seems more likely that they will continue to tolerate other ideas of God but hold to their own faith in the divine Name as taught by their *gurus* and scriptures.

Sikh temple tower commemorating martyrs, Amritsar

CHECK YOUR READING

Who were the Aryans?

What did the Indus people believe?

Who are Shiva and his wife?

What is an *avatar*?

What is Pantheism?

How long was India under British rule?

What was Juggernaut?

What did the Brahmo Samaj teach?

What do you know about Gandhi?

What are the two main divisions of the Jains?

What do Jain vegetarians practise?

What is the most famous Jain teaching?

Who were the Magi?

What happened when the Moslems invaded Persia?

Where did the Zoroastrians emigrate?

What does Parsi mean?

Why are the Parsis influential?

What do they say about other religions?

What did the Sikh leader Arjun do?

Who founded the Sikh inner circle of initiates?

What is their special dress?

Describe the Sikh relations with British rule.

What happened at the Partition of India in 1947?

What have Sikhs done since then?

INDIAN RELIGIONS AT CENSUS OF 1961	
Hindus	366 million
Moslems	47 ,,
Christians	10 ,,
Sikhs	6 ,,
Buddhists	3½ ,,
Jains	1½ ,,
Parsis	115,000

INDIAN RELIGIONS

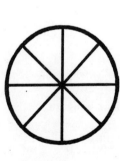

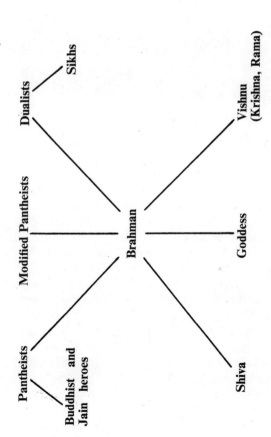

Dualists — Sikhs

Modified Pantheists

Pantheists — Buddhist and Jain heroes

Brahman

Vishnu (Krishna, Rama)

Goddess

Shiva

BUDDHIST EXPANSION

Gautama the Buddha died in the fifth century B.C. His teachings had some success and there were orders of monks that followed him. But a great spur to the spread of the religion came from the emperor Ashoka, 200 years later.

The Greek warrior Alexander the Great had invaded the Punjab in 326 B.C. and his successors were in contact with a rising Indian dynasty led by the Maurya kings. The most famous of these was Ashoka Maurya, who was crowned in 265 B.C. We can date Buddhism and other Indian religions from his time, not only through his links with the Greeks, but also because Ashoka put out decrees engraved on stone slabs and pillars, many of which still exist.

H. G. Wells called Ashoka one of the six greatest rulers of history. He was certainly one of the noblest. After an early war against a neighbouring tribe, Ashoka was revolted by the slaughter and vowed never

Buddhist temple, Thailand

161

Burmese monks with begging bowls

to engage in war again. He became a Buddhist, some say a monk, and spread its teachings. Not only did he forbid taking human life but taking animal life also, even for food in the royal palace. He built hospitals for men and animals, made rest-houses, dug wells and planted shade trees.

Ashoka also sent out missions to spread Buddhism, west, east and south. He had stone inscriptions made, praising 'the Buddha, the Law and the Order'. He built memorials at the places of the birth, enlightenment and death of the Buddha. This encouraged pilgrimages, and some of his memorials are still to be seen. Ashoka made Buddhism much more attractive to ordinary people, as well as monks, and told them to visit the temples every week.

It is said that Ashoka's son, a monk, took Buddhism to Ceylon, and a slab of rock underneath a cliff is still shown there where this missionary first slept. Soon the king of Ceylon had accepted the religion, and later immense monastery buildings were made, ruins of which remain today. The Ceylonese Buddhists wanted relics of the Buddha, and in due course claimed to have his collar-bone and tooth, which are enshrined today in golden caskets, and placed in huge conical buildings called dagobas or pagodas.

The people of Burma claim that two missionaries went to them from Ashoka and that they have eight hairs of the Buddha, in the Golden Pagoda in Rangoon. Certainly Buddhism went there in the early centuries, and this is today one of the strongest Buddhist countries. Buddhism went on to the other countries of South-east Asia: Siam (Thailand), Cambodia and Laos. These are the lands of Southern Buddhism, where it is claimed that Buddhism is strongest and in its purest form. There are fine Buddhist monuments in Java also, but this country later became overrun by Moslems and

162

CHART OF BUDDHIST SECTS

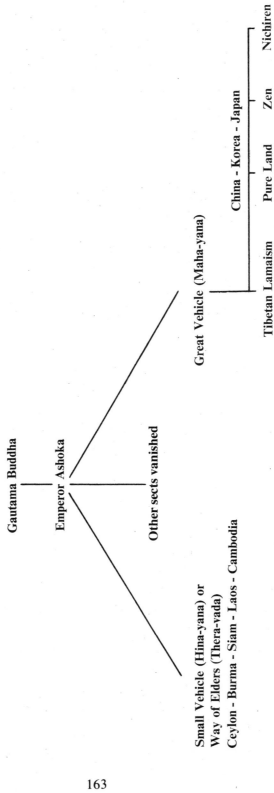

Gautama Buddha

Emperor Ashoka

Other sects vanished

Small Vehicle (Hina-yana) or
Way of Elders (Thera-vada)
Ceylon - Burma - Siam - Laos - Cambodia

Great Vehicle (Maha-yana)

China - Korea - Japan

Tibetan Lamaism

Pure Land

Zen

Nichiren

Buddhism as a practised religion disappeared.

At an early date Buddhism divided into several parts. It is said that on the death of Gautama a Council was held at which the monks recited the rules of discipline from the first of the Three Baskets (see page 121). Then a hundred years later another Council met to discuss differences in monkish rules. Some monks had been taking more than one meal a day, drinking liquor and taking money. Only 2,000 of the 12,000 monks insisted on the stricter rules and broke away to form the Southern Buddhists.

A different version is given by the Northern Buddhists. They say the other monks were only intent on their own salvation by the monkish life, but they themselves wanted a broader way which would be open to all men. So they call themselves the Great Vehicle (Maha-yana) of salvation for all men, while the others are the Little Vehicle (Hina-yana). But the Southerns prefer the title Way of the Elders (Thera-vada). The teachings of the Great Vehicle are in the Lotus Scripture (see page 122), where salvation is offered to all those who by faith call upon the gracious Buddha. Many other Buddhas appear there, and also gracious Beings of Enlightenment (Bodhi-sattvas) who have put off their own entry into Nirvana till all other beings are saved (see page 34).

It was this Great Vehicle teaching that took Buddhism to the countries north of India. In the first century A.D. Buddhist monks crossed into China, and over the centuries there were journeys to take scriptures, images and relics. At first the Chinese did not take to Buddhism, since young men were taken away into monasteries, and the teaching of rebirth went against the Chinese practice of ancestor worship. But in time the peaceful missionaries won, and Buddhism became one of the Three Ways of China.

In the sixth century A.D. Buddhism began its success in Tibet. The gods of the native religion (Bon) were taken as guardians of Buddhism, and finally Buddhism took full control. Its great monasteries ruled the country. Tibetan monks are in two orders, the Yellow Hats and the Red Hats. The Yellow Hats are the rulers. The heads of their monasteries are 'lamas' or abbots, and their chief is the Dalai Lama whose traditional home is the great Potala Palace in Lhasa. Each great Lama is taken as the rebirth of a Buddha or Being of Enlightenment. The Dalai Lama is the reincarnation of Kwanyin (Chenresi), the Being of Compassion of the Lotus Scripture.

Buddhism has suffered in China and Tibet under Communist rule. Many monasteries are deserted, though some are preserved as national monuments. There is an officially sponsored Chinese Buddhist Association. The Dalai Lama fled from Tibet to India in 1959, but his people are still loyal to him, though many of the younger ones have been taken away to China.

Buddhism spread from China to Vietnam, Korea and Japan. Japanese developments are most interesting. For a long time Buddhism took control of most Shinto temples and formed a Twofold Shinto, which was dissolved in the nineteenth century. There are over a dozen Japanese Buddhist sects. The largest are the Pure Land, which teach faith in Amida Buddha, the Lord of the Western Paradise (see page 122). Against this Nichiren, a reformer, objected and preached a return to Gautama Buddha, but still the glorified Buddha of the Lotus Scripture. The most famous sect is Zen (see page 132). Zen started in China, and is a mixture of Buddhism and Chinese Tao. It teaches 'meditation' (Chinese *chan*) as a means to 'enlightenment'. It discards many scriptures, though it uses the Lotus Scripture in recitations. Zen adapts itself to daily life and work: fencing, archery, flowers.

Buddhism is powerful in Japan today, and its strength is the closest of the Northern Buddhists to that of Burma and Siam. They seek to follow 'the Way of the Buddhas'.

The Dalai Lama

165

CHINESE THREE WAYS

We have seen that Confucius was not a religious teacher primarily, yet religion was essential to him as to most Chinese. Belief in Heaven (Shang Ti or Tien) was the guide of life to Confucius and his followers. The religion of ancient China was represented by the emperor who sacrificed to Heaven at the different seasons of the year (see page 36). Throughout the country ordinary people then sacrificed to the local spirits, and gave special reverence to Heaven and Earth and the ancestors.

Confucius was honoured by scholars, and they came to direct the state rites, and so these and the offerings to the ancestors came to be called Confucianism. Other great

Taoist
Judge of
Future
Life

teachers like Mencius (Meng Tse) enlarged the teachings of Confucius, and taught their duties to rulers and people alike. Mencius told a ruler, 'Love and protect the common people, and none can prevent you from becoming a true king.' Like most Chinese teachers, Mencius had a great dislike for war, and it had been a tradition to regard the scholar as the best of men and soldiers as inferior.

After the Classic of the Way (Tao Te Ching) other books sought to develop its teachings. They taught of the Yin and Yang, symbolised in the two halves of the circle. The union of these two shows the harmony of the universe (see page 35).

Later Taoist writers developed the notion of living according to nature; they were vegetarians, living on plants and water. Some of them were primitive scientists, trying to discover how nature worked. But others went astray in a search for immortality by magical means. Some practised kinds of yoga, controlling breath and motion. But others tried to fly through the air and dissolve their bodies.

Taoism declined into a system of magic, in which the priests sold long-life pills and medicines that were as much based on fanciful notions as real curative properties. Taoist societies were often secret, and a trouble to governments. The Boxer Rising in 1900 was a Taoist society of 'Righteous Energy'. Here the peaceful teaching of the early Way was almost forgotten.

Taoism also mixed with Buddhism, to

take control of funeral ceremonies, and on a better level to produce the Chan or Zen types of meditation.

In modern times a reform of Chinese religion was overdue. Early Christian missionaries deplored the many idols, and these have since been mostly destroyed. The Jesuits, however, for long claimed that the reverence paid to ancestors was not religious, and that the Confucians were some of the leaders of civilization.

Under Communism all religions have suffered. Confucius himself has been called feudal, though his grave was repaired in 1962. There is an official Chinese Taoist Association, and it is said that 'half the soul of China is Taoist'. The Classic of the Way is revered and read. The common people still have tablets of Heaven and Earth and ancestors in their homes. The scholars read the Classics, and the Way may still triumph by taking the lowest path.

Hall of
Classics
near Confucian
temple,
Peking

167

SHINTO MIXTURES

After its ancient isolation Shinto was over-shadowed by the coming of Buddhism in the sixth century A.D. The new religion had literature, priests, organization and superior culture. After an early setback Buddhism obtained official favour when Prince Shotoku adopted it. Permission was sought from the Sun-goddess herself, Amaterasu, for building Buddhist temples and images. She is said to have replied that the sun was identical with a Buddha of light. After that all the Shinto gods were taken as manifestations of Buddhas who were the real originals.

Most Shinto temples were taken over by Buddhist priests, and images introduced. Only a few national shrines, such as Isé, were preserved free of Buddhism. This

Mixed or Twofold Shinto lasted till 1868. But before this there had been writers, such as Motoori and Hirata, who urged a Shinto revival, and wanted to reject both the culture and the religion that came from China and India.

Part of the revolt against Buddhism was

A Japanese home shrine

168

Heian Shrine, Kyoto

political. After the early European traders had visited Japan, the country was closed in 1600 and dictators were the real rulers, with the emperor kept in seclusion. Buddhist leaders sided with the dictators, so when there was a reaction Buddhism suffered. In 1868 the emperor came to power again; Japan was opened to foreign trade, Shinto was restored and Buddhism was persecuted. But Christian missions came in and demanded freedom of religion. Buddhism benefited by this too, and came to be recognised as a Japanese religion, though still separate from Shinto.

Two kinds of Shinto were recognised: State or Sanctuary Shinto, and Sect Shinto. The many sanctuaries ranged from tiny wayside shrines to ancient temples in great parks with long avenues of stone arches. Until 1945 all these were said to belong to the State, and all citizens and school children were supposed to bow at these shrines as a sign of respect to the emperor and state. This caused great hardship to Buddhists and Christians if they had to bow at some shrine containing Shinto symbols. But after 1945 the State connexion with the shrines was severed, and only the great temples, such as Isé, receive State support.

The Shinto Sects arose in the nineteenth century, and show the influence of Buddhism and Christianity as well as Shinto. Some give modern forms of ancient Shinto practices, especially in pilgrimages and mountain climbing. But others are more like churches, with central organization, temples, houses and schools. The members work freely for the good of the society.

These sects have historical founders; the most popular, Tenri-kyo, was founded by a woman, Miki, in 1839. They usually teach healing of sickness by faith, and stress the importance of prayer and purity of heart.

With the Shinto sects, the ancient Shinto shrines, Buddhism and Christianity, Japan has been called 'a laboratory of religion'.

169

AFRICAN CHANGES

Old maps of Africa, if they showed any sketch of religion at all, would paint nearly all the continent 'pagan' south of the Sahara. North Africa has been Moslem for a thousand years, and Abyssinia Christian for even longer. But the tropical and southern areas were neither Moslem nor Christian till modern times.

Even fifty years ago the number of Christians in Africa would be reckoned at a little over 5 million, nearly all in Abyssinia and Egypt, with a few in Algeria. But in 1962 an authoritative survey reckoned 53 million Christians in Africa, out of a total population of about 230 millions. These 53 million Christians were divided into 29 million Roman Catholics, 19 million Protestants and 5 million Copts and Orthodox.

This was the result of little over a century of Christian missionary work, which had borne greater fruits in Africa than anywhere else. Not only are there those who have

official connexions with the Churches, but many others who are not Church members are indirectly influenced by the Church. Most of the schools were run by missions, and educated the political leaders who have taken their countries out of colonialism into independence.

At the same time Islam has also spread widely in modern Africa. For centuries it remained static in the desert and Sudan areas of the north. But the opening up of Africa, with roads and railways, has meant great increase of trade, and with trade has come the Islamic religion. No one knows how many Moslems there are in tropical Africa. Their numbers vary in different countries; strong in Northern Nigeria and Senegal, weak in Eastern Nigeria and Ghana.

The reason for this rapidly changing religious picture of Africa is the breakdown of old societies, and the rise of new forms of education and government. Then the new religions, Christianity and Islam, have great advantages. They are universal religions, with history and scriptures. The old African religions had no scriptures and their history was little more than legend. They were tied to village life and did not fit easily into the new life of towns, mines and ports. An international brotherhood, and religious teaching which surpasses time and space, has obvious advantages.

The old religion remains, but it is in the villages and more remote places that it is strongest. One way in which traditional African religion showed its power was within the new religions themselves. Many Chris-

African Christian prophetess

tian sects broke away from the larger churches, over 2,000 in South Africa. These were assertions of spiritual independence, not so much political as reactions against the formality of church life. New Prophets have arisen, teaching healing by faith, and adapting African music and dancing to Christian purposes.

Islam and Christianity are rivals for the soul of Africa. But in the main they are tolerant of each other, and they take their converts not so much from each other as from the declining paganism. But in all forms of its religion, Africa shows trust in God not only in formal prayer but in daily life and as a help in trouble.

CHECK YOUR READING

Who was Alexander the Great?
When did Ashoka live?
Why did he become a Buddhist?
How did he publish his decrees?
What did Ashoka teach?
Who took Buddhism to Ceylon?
Which are the lands of Southern Buddhism?
Why did Buddhists divide?
What does the Great Vehicle teach?
What do you know of Buddhism in Tibet?
Name some Japanese Buddhist sects.
What did Mencius teach?
What are Yang and Yin?
Describe the development of Taoism.
What is the present state of religion in China?

What is Twofold Shinto?
What happened after Japan was closed to Europe?
Name the two kinds of Shinto.
What do the Shinto sects teach?
How was Buddhism established in Japan?
Who led the revival of Shinto?
Where are the oldest Christian churches in Africa?
How many Christians are there in Africa today?
How is Islam spreading in Africa?
Why is the old paganism declining?
Why is Christianity growing in Africa?

University Chapel, Ibadan, Nigeria

171

EXPANDING RELIGIONS

Some of the world's greatest religions have been spread by missionaries far beyond the lands where they had their origin. The reason why they went abroad was that they felt that their teaching was the highest truth, and that it was suitable for all men and women. The three great missionary religions are, in historical order, Buddhism, Christianity and Islam.

Some religions are strictly for one nation. Such are the Parsis who do not admit members of other religions to their temples. The Jews, who once taught religion to the Mediterranean world, became closed in upon themselves and left the teaching of religion to the world to Christianity and Islam. Shinto in Japan is a national faith, though for a time under the emperors it was said to be destined for the whole world. Tribal religions in Africa, and the forests of South America and eastern Asia, are limited to members of those tribes.

Confucian and Taoist ideas spread from China to Japan, but there was no real mission. It used to be said that the Hindu religion was for those born into a Hindu caste, but the Ramakrishna Mission (see page 154) now spreads Hindu teachings abroad and so does the Theosophical Society. The Jains and Sikhs have remained Indian though in theory their teaching is for anybody.

Islam is one of the greatest missionary religions, and in less than a century from its foundation it extended from Spain to India. Today its great strength is in North Africa and the Middle East. After halting for centuries, Islam is advancing again, especially in West and East Africa.

Buddhism began in India but it has only a few followers there now. It soon spread over South-east Asia and later through China to farthest Korea and Japan. In modern times Buddhism has gone to some of the Pacific Islands, and the western coast of America, and has sent missions to other parts of America and Europe.

Christianity began in Palestine and, despite persecution, it rapidly spread across Europe and the Near East. Missions went even to China in the early centuries, though they disappeared. In the age of discovery, in the sixteenth century, missions again went to the Far East, and to America and Africa. The modern missionary movement, in the nineteenth and twentieth centuries, has spread Christianity into nearly every country in the world.

Religions have been persecuted again: Jews in Germany under the Nazis, and all religions under Communism. Yet even today the Russian Orthodox Church claims 30 million members, and there are other Churches and religions also in the Soviet Union and China.

Attendance at Churches has declined in some countries in Europe, yet we must look at the World Church. Christianity has gained more members in the twentieth century than at any previous time in its history. It has more than twice as many members as any other religion; its numbers have doubled in the past eighty years, more than the growth in world population during that period.

To modern men and women the religions of the world offer their teaching as ways of understanding the meaning of human life and the universe. The forms of religion are different, and they may change in various countries and ages, but as long as men are men they will seek to discover the final meaning of life and the highest ideals for conduct.

INDEX

Maccabees, 19, 56, 89, 140
Magi, wise men, 23, 56, 157
magic, 45, 166
Mahabharata, epic, 108
Mahavira, 29, 48, 69 f., 77, 112 f., 157
Mahayana Buddhists, 124, 163 f.
Mahdi, coming one, 148
Mahomet, *see* Mohammed
Maimonides, 135
Manu, Laws of, 108, 111
Mary, mother of Jesus, 21, 56, 61, 101, 104
Mecca, 10, 12, 60, 74, 100, 148
meditation, 26, 32, 34, 132, 164
Mencius, 166
Mesopotamia, 46 f., 87, 140, 147 f., 152
Messiah, Christ, 20, 56 f., 90, 95
Methodists, 144
mezuzah, doorpost box, 16
Middle Way, 72, 123, 128
Mikado, emperor, 36
Milinda, king, 122 ff.
minaret, 12, 13, 15
miracles, healing, 57
missions, 138, 142, 145, 162, 169, 170, 172
Mithra, God, 64, 115
Mogul empire, 154
Mohammed, 14, 16, 50, 60 f., 67, 87, 100 f., 135 f., 147
monasteries, monks, 32, 34, 70, 72, 102, 120, 125, 157, 164
Monophysites, 143
morality, conduct, 29, 30, 32, 80, 97, 99, 104, 114, 115 f., 126
Mormons, 144
Moses, 52 ff., 66, 88
Moslems, 10, 12, 14, 28, 30, 102, 157, *and see* Islam
mosque, 12, 16
mother goddess, 28, 46, 152
Motoori, 132, 168
Mount Sinai, 53, 94
muezzin, prayer crier, 12
mummy, 46 f.

Nanak, 31, 41, 74, 78, 117 f., 158
Nero, emperor, 96, 143
New Stone Age, 46
Nicene Creed, 135, 143
Nichiren, 163 f.
Nigeria, 12, 150, 170, 171
Nihongi, chronicles, 131
nirvana, going out, 70, 72, 113, 122, 124, 164
Nonconformists, 144, *and see* Free Churches
non-violence, 29, 113, 154, 157

Old Stone Age, 44 f.
Om, Aum, invocation, 26

Omar, caliph, 147 f.
Orthodox Churches, 21, 143, 172
Orthodox Jews, 17, 142
outcastes, 154, *and see* Caste

pagan, 11, 170
pagodas, 32 f., 162
Pakistan, 148, 158
Palestine, 46, 48, 52, 56, 59, 64, 140, 142
pantheism, all is God, 154
paper, invented, 126, 148
papyrus, 94 f.
paradise, *see* Heaven
Parsis, 30, 64, 115 f., 136, 157
Passover, 19, 23, 53
paten, plate, 22
Pater Noster, 21
Paul, 56, 95, 143
Peking, 35 f., 167
Pentateuch, *see* Torah
Pentecost, Whitsun, 23, 58
Persia, Iran, 30, 38, 46, 64, 148, 157
Pharisees, 140
pilgrimage, 62, 70, 136
Plymouth Brethren, 144
polytheism, many gods, 26, 39, 106 f.
Pope, 143 f.
prayer, *see* Worship
prayer-beads, rosary, 21, 26, 29, 30, 34
prayer-flags and wheels, 34, 136
Presbyterians, 21, 144
primitive people, 44
printing, 79, 122 f., 126
Protestants, *see* Reformation
Pure Land, Buddhists, 34, 164
pyramids, 47, 52

Quakers, Friends, 23, 144

rabbi, teacher, 18, 140 f.
Rama, hero and god, 68, 77, 111, 152
Ramadan, fast month, 136
Ramakrishna, holy man, 154, 172
Ramanuja, 154
Ramayana, epic, 108
Rangoon, 33, 162
rebirth, *see* Reincarnation
Reform Jews, 17, 142
Reformation, Protestant, 144
Reformed Churches, 21, 144
reincarnation, 31, 34, 107, 110, 113, 117, 122 f., 152
relics, 16, 33, 34, 72, 162
resurrection, 23, 58, 61
Roman Catholics, 21, 144 f., 170
Roman empire, 56, 87, 94, 140, 143
rosary, *see* Prayer-beads

175